# Federal Benefits for Veterans and Dependents

## 2007 Edition

## Department of Veterans Affairs

**Office of Public Affairs (80D)**
**810 Vermont Ave., N.W.**
**Washington, DC 20420**

# U.S. GOVERNMENT OFFICIAL EDITION

## Use of ISBN

This is the official U.S. government edition of this publication and is herein identified to certify its authenticity.  Use of the 0-16 ISBN prefix is for U.S. Government Printing Office Official Editions only.  The Superintendent of Documents of the U.S. Government Printing Office requests that any reprinted edition clearly be labeled as a copy of the authentic work with a new ISBN.

## Legal Status and Use of Seals and Logos

The seal of the Department of Veterans Affairs authenticates the 2007 edition of Federal Benefits for Veterans and Dependents as the official summary of benefits that have been separately promulgated under Federal regulations established under the Federal Register Act. Under the provisions of 38 Code of Federal Regulations 1.9(f), it is prohibited to use the official seal, replicas, reproductions, or embossed seals of the Department of Veterans Affairs on any republication of this material without the express, written permission of the Secretary or Deputy Secretary of Veterans Affairs.  Any person using official seals and logos of the Department of Veterans Affairs in a manner inconsistent with the provisions of 38 Code of Federal Regulations 1.9 may be subject to the penalties specified in 18 United States Code 506, 701, or 1017 as applicable.

---


For sale by the Superintendent of Documents, U.S. Government Printing Office
Internet: bookstore.gpo.gov  Phone: toll free (866) 512-1800; DC area (202) 512-1800
Fax: (202) 512-2104  Mail: Stop IDCC, Washington, DC 20402-0001

ISBN 978-0-16-078005-9

# Contents

# Prologue

During the Civil War, President Abraham Lincoln affirmed our nation's commitment "to care for him who shall have borne the battle, and for his widow and his orphan."  His eloquent words live on today as the motto of the Department of Veterans Affairs, the federal agency responsible for honoring our nation's debt of gratitude to America's patriots.

Over the years, federal benefits for veterans have evolved to meet their changing needs. For example, VA has established a "seamless transition" program to ensure that servicemembers returning from combat in Afghanistan and Iraq in support of the Global War on Terror receive the information they need about VA benefits and services before they leave the military and begin the transition to civilian life.

While much of our immediate attention focuses on our new generation of veterans, we certainly have not forgotten veterans who served in past wars.  This publication is intended as a reference guide for all of our nation's veterans, their spouses and family members, and those who help veterans access VA benefits and services.

It is said that the measure of a nation is gauged by the way its people honor their defenders.  The decision to step forward to support and defend the Constitution, serving in harm's way when necessary, exacts a great toll.  Yet our veterans do not hesitate to serve and bear the cost of freedom for all.  In everything that we do here at VA, we strive to honor veterans – our nation's defenders – as they have honored us through their service and sacrifice.

Jim Nicholson
Secretary of Veterans Affairs

# Introduction

Veterans of the United States armed forces may be eligible for a broad range of programs and services provided by the federal Department of Veterans Affairs (VA). These benefits are legislated in Title 38 of the United States Code. This booklet contains a summary of these benefits effective Jan. 1, 2007. For additional information, visit the VA Web page at http://www.va.gov/.

La versión en español de este folleto se encuentra disponible en formato Adobe Acrobat a través de el link: http://www.va.gov/opa/feature/index.asp.

## General Eligibility

Eligibility for most VA benefits is based upon discharge from active military service under other than dishonorable conditions. Active service means full-time service, other than active duty for training, as a member of the Army, Navy, Air Force, Marine Corps, Coast Guard, or as a commissioned officer of the Public Health Service, Environmental Science Services Administration or National Oceanic and Atmospheric Administration, or its predecessor, the Coast and Geodetic Survey. Generally, men and women veterans with similar service may be entitled to the same VA benefits.

Dishonorable and bad conduct discharges issued by general courts-martial may bar VA benefits. Veterans in prison and parolees must contact a VA regional office to determine eligibility. VA benefits will not be provided to any veteran or dependent wanted for an outstanding felony warrant.

### Certain VA Benefits Require Wartime Service

Certain VA benefits require service during wartime. Under the law, VA recognizes these war periods:

**Mexican Border Period:** May 9, 1916, through April 5, 1917, for veterans who served in Mexico, on its borders or in adjacent waters.

**World War I:** April 6, 1917, through Nov. 11, 1918; for veterans who served in Russia, April 6, 1917, through April 1, 1920; extended through July 1, 1921, for veterans who had at least one day of service between April 6, 1917, and Nov. 11, 1918.

**World War II:** Dec. 7, 1941, through Dec. 31, 1946.

**Korean War:** June 27, 1950, through Jan. 31, 1955.

**Vietnam War:** Aug. 5, 1964 (Feb. 28, 1961, for veterans who served "in country" before Aug. 5, 1964), through May 7, 1975.

**Gulf War:** Aug. 2, 1990, through a date to be set by law or Presidential Proclamation.

# Important Documents Needed for Verifying and Processing VA Claims

Veterans seeking a VA benefit for the first time must submit a copy of their service discharge form (DD-214, DD-215, or for World War II veterans, a WD form), which documents service dates and type of discharge, or give their full name, military service number, and branch and dates of service. The veteran's service discharge form should be kept in a safe location accessible to the veteran and next of kin or designated representative.

The following documents will be needed for claims processing related to a veteran's death:

1. Veteran's marriage certificate for claims of a surviving spouse or children.

2. Veteran's death certificate if the veteran did not die in a VA health care facility.

3. Children's birth certificates or adoption papers to determine children's benefits.

4. Veteran's birth certificate to determine parents' benefits.

# Acronyms

ACE – Automated Certificate of Eligibility
ALS – Amytrophic Lateral Sclerosis
CHAMPVA – Civilian Health and Medical Program of VA
C&P – Compensation and Pension
CRDP – Concurrent Retirement and Disability Payments
CRSC – Combat-Related Special Compensation
CWT – Compensated Work Therapy
CZTE – Combat Zone Tax Exclusion
DIC – Dependency and Indemnity Compensation
DOD -- Department of Defense
FHA – Federal Housing Administration
FSGLI – Family Servicemembers' Group Life Insurance
HUD – Department of Housing and Urban Development
IRR – Individual Ready Reserve
MGIB – Montgomery GI Bill
MIA – Missing in Action
NPRC – National Personnel Records Center
NSLI – National Service Life Insurance
OEF – Operation Enduring Freedom
OIF – Operation Iraqi Freedom
OPM – Office of Personnel Management
POW -- Prisoners of War
PTSD – Post-Traumatic Stress Disorder
RIF – Reduction in Force
SAH – Specially Adapted Housing
SBA – Small Business Administration
SSI – Supplemental Security Income
S-DVI – Service-Disabled Veterans' Insurance
SGLI – Servicemembers' Group Life Insurance
SSB – Special Separation Benefits
TAP – Transition Assistance Program
TSGLI – Traumatic Servicemembers' Group Life Insurance
TWA – Transcontinental and Western Air, Inc.
USCIS – U.S. Citizenship and Immigration Services
USDA – U.S. Department of Agriculture
VA – Department of Veterans Affairs
VEAP – Veterans Educational Assistance Program
VEOA – Veterans' Employment Opportunities Act
VGLI – Veterans' Group Life Insurance
VHA – Veterans Health Administration
VMET – Verification of Military Experience and Training
VMLI – Veterans' Mortgage Life Insurance
VR&E – Vocational Rehabilitation and Employment
VSI – Voluntary Separation Incentives
WAAC – Women's Army Auxiliary Corps
WASPs – Women Air Force Service Pilots

# Chapter 1

# VA Health Care

*Enrollment, Priority Groups, Veteran Health Registries, Readjustment Counseling Services, Prosthetic and Sensory Aids, Mental Health Care Treatment, Outpatient Dental Treatment, Outpatient Pharmacy Services, Nursing Home Care*

VA operates the nation's largest integrated health care system with more than 1,400 sites of care, including hospitals, community clinics, nursing homes, domiciliaries, readjustment counseling centers, and various other facilities. For additional information on VA health care, visit: http://www.va.gov/health/.

## Enrollment

For most veterans, entry into the VA health care system begins by applying for enrollment. To apply, complete VA Form 10-10EZ, Application for Health Benefits, which may be obtained from any VA health care facility or regional benefits office, on line at http://www.va.gov/1010ez.htm or by calling 1-877-222-VETS (8387). Once enrolled, veterans can receive health care at VA health care facilities anywhere in the country.

Veterans enrolled in the VA health care system are afforded privacy rights under federal law. VA's Notice of Privacy Practices, which describes how VA may use and disclose veterans' medical information, is also available on line at http://www.va.gov/vhapublications/ViewPublication.asp?pub_ID=1089

The following three categories of veterans are not required to enroll, but are urged to do so to permit better planning of health resources:

1. Veterans with a service-connected disability of 50 percent or more.
2. Veterans seeking care for a disability the military determined was incurred or aggravated in  the line of duty, but which VA has not yet rated, within 12 months of discharge.
3. Veterans seeking care for a service-connected disability only.

## Priority Groups

During enrollment, each veteran is assigned to a priority group.  VA uses priority groups to balance demand for VA health care enrollment with resources. Changes in available resources may reduce the number of priority groups VA can enroll. If this occurs, VA will publicize the changes and notify affected enrollees. A description of priority groups follows:

**Group 1:** Veterans with service-connected disabilities rated 50 percent or more and/or veterans determined by VA to be unemployable due to service-connected conditions.

**Group 2:** Veterans with service-connected disabilities rated 30 or 40 percent.

**Group 3:** Veterans with service-connected disabilities rated 10 and 20 percent, veterans who are former Prisoners of War (POW) or were awarded a Purple Heart medal, veterans awarded special eligibility for disabilities incurred in treatment or participation in a VA Vocational Rehabilitation program, and veterans whose discharge was for a disability incurred or aggravated in the line of duty.

**Group 4:** Veterans receiving aid and attendance or housebound benefits and/or veterans determined by VA to be catastrophically disabled. Some veterans in this group may be responsible for co-pays.

**Group 5:** Veterans receiving VA pension benefits or eligible for Medicaid programs, and non service-connected veterans and noncompensable, zero percent service-connected veterans whose gross annual household income and net worth are below the established

VA means test thresholds.

**Group 6:** Veterans of the Mexican border period or World War I; veterans seeking care solely for certain conditions associated with exposure to radiation or exposure to herbicides while serving in Vietnam; for any illness associated with combat service in a war after the Gulf War or during a period of hostility after Nov. 11, 1998; for any illness associated with participation in tests conducted by the Department of Defense (DOD) as part of Project 112/Project SHAD; and veterans with zero percent service-connected disabilities who are receiving disability compensation benefits.

**Group 7:** Non service-connected veterans and non-compensable, zero percent service-connected veterans with gross annual household income above VA's national means test threshold and below VA's geographic means test threshold, or with gross annual household income below both the VA national threshold and the VA geographically based threshold, but whose income plus net worth exceeds VA's ceiling (currently $80,000) who agree to pay co-pays.

**Group 8:** All other non service-connected veterans and zero percent, non-compensable service-connected veterans who agree to pay co-pays. (Note: Effective Jan. 17, 2003, VA no longer enrolls new veterans in priority group 8).

# Special Access to Care

**Service Disabled Veterans:** Veterans who are 50 percent or more disabled from service-connected conditions, unemployable due to service-connected conditions, or receiving care for a service-connected disability receive priority in scheduling of hospital or outpatient medical appointments.

**Combat Veterans:** Veterans who served in combat locations during active military service after Nov. 11, 1998, are eligible for free health care services for conditions potentially related to combat service for two years following separation from active duty. For additional information call 1-877-222-VETS (8387).

# Financial Assessment

Most veterans not receiving VA disability compensation or pension payments must provide information on their gross annual household income and net worth to determine whether they are below the annually adjusted financial thresholds.

This financial assessment includes all household income and net worth, including Social Security, retirement pay, unemployment insurance, interest and dividends, workers' compensation, black lung benefits and any other income. Also considered are assets such as the market value of property that is not the primary residence, stocks, bonds, notes, individual retirement accounts, bank deposits, savings accounts and cash.

VA also compares veterans' financial assessment with geographically based income thresholds. If the veteran's gross annual household income is above VA's national means test threshold and below VA's geographic means test threshold, or is below both the VA national threshold and the VA geographically based threshold, but their gross annual household income plus net worth exceeds VA's ceiling (currently $80,000) the veteran is eligible for an 80-percent reduction in inpatient co-pay rates.

## VA Medical Services and Supplies Requiring Veterans to Make Co-Pays

Some veterans must make co-pays to receive VA health care.

**Inpatient Care:** Veterans with income above the means test threshold and below VA's geographically based income threshold (Priority Group 7) are responsible for paying 20 percent of the Medicare deductible for the first 90 days of inpatient hospital care during any 365-day period. For each additional 90 days, they are charged 10 percent of the Medicare deductible. In addition, they are charged $2 a day for hospital care.

Non service-connected veterans and non-compensable, zero percent service-connected veterans with gross annual household income above the VA national and geographic income thresholds will be charged the full Medicare deductible for the first 90 days of care during any 365-day period and $10 per day. For each additional 90 days, they are charged one half of the Medicare deductible and the per diem charge.

**Extended Care:** With certain exceptions, veterans must pay co-pays for extended care. The co-pay amount is based on each veteran's financial situation and is determined upon application for extended care services.

**Medication:** Most veterans are currently charged $8 for each 30-day or less supply of medication provided by VA for treatment of conditions that are not service-connected.

**Outpatient Care:** A three-tiered co-pay system is used for all outpatient services. The co-pay is $15 for a primary care visit and $50 for some specialized care. Certain services are not charged a co-pay.

## Outpatient Visits Not Requiring Co-Pays

Co-pays do not apply to publicly announced VA health fairs or outpatient visits solely for preventive screening and/or immunizations, such as immunizations for influenza and pneumococcal, or screening for hypertension, hepatitis C, tobacco, alcohol, hyperlipidemia, breast cancer, cervical cancer, colorectal cancer by fecal occult blood testing, education about the risks and benefits of prostate cancer screening, and smoking cessation counseling (individual and group). Laboratory, flat film radiology, and electrocardiograms are also exempt from co-pays.

## Private Health Insurance Billing

VA is required to bill private health insurance providers for medical care, supplies and prescriptions provided for treatment of veterans' non service-connected conditions. Generally, VA cannot bill Medicare, but can bill Medicare supplemental health insurance for covered services.

All veterans applying for VA medical care are required to provide information on their health insurance coverage, including coverage provided under policies of their spouses. Veterans are not responsible for paying any remaining balance of VA's insurance claim not paid or covered by their health insurance, and any payment received by VA may be used to offset "dollar for dollar" a veteran's VA co-pay responsibility.

## Some Travel Costs to Receive VA Medical Care May be Reimbursed by VA

Certain veterans may be reimbursed for travel costs to receive VA medical care. Reimbursement is paid at $.11 per mile -- or $.17 per mile if called for a repeat Compensation & Pension (C&P) exam -- and is subject to a deductible of $3 for each one-way trip and an $18-per-month maximum payment. Two exceptions to the deductible are travel for C&P exam and special modes of transportation, such as an ambulance or a specially equipped van.

**Eligibility:** Payments may be made to the following:

1. Veterans whose service-connected disabilities are rated 30 percent or more.
2. Veterans traveling for treatment of a service connected condition.
3. Veterans who receive a VA pension.
4. Veterans traveling for scheduled compensation or pension examinations.
5. Veterans whose gross household income does not exceed the maximum annual VA pension.
6. Veterans whose medical condition requires a special mode of transportation, if they are unable to defray the costs and travel is pre-authorized. Advance authorization is not required in an emergency if a delay would be hazardous to life or health.

# VA Medical Programs

## Veteran Health Registries

Certain veterans can participate in a VA health registry and receive free medical examinations, including laboratory and other diagnostic tests deemed necessary by an examining clinician. VA maintains health registries to provide special health examinations and health-related information. To participate, contact the nearest VA health care facility or visit http://www.va.gov/environagents/.

**Gulf War Registry:** For veterans who served in the Gulf War and Operation Iraqi Freedom (OIF).

**Depleted Uranium Registries:** VA maintains two registries for veterans possibly exposed to depleted uranium. The first is for veterans who served in the Gulf War, including Operation Iraqi Freedom. The second is for veterans who served elsewhere, including Bosnia and Afghanistan.

**Agent Orange Registry:** For veterans possibly exposed to dioxin or other toxic substances in herbicides used during the Vietnam War, while serving in Korea in 1968 or 1969, or as a result of testing, transporting, or spraying herbicides for military purposes.

**Ionizing Radiation Registry:** For veterans possibly exposed to atomic radiation during the following activities: atmospheric detonation of a nuclear device; occupation of Hiroshima or Nagasaki from Aug. 6, 1945, through July 1, 1946; internment as a prisoner of war in Japan during World War II; serving in official military duties at the gaseous diffusion plants at Paducah, Ky.; Portsmouth, Ohio; or the K-25 area at Oak Ridge, Tenn., for at least 250 days before Feb. 1, 1992, or in Longshot, Milrow or Cannikin underground nuclear tests at Amchitka Island, Alaska, before Jan. 1, 1974; or treatment with nasopharyngeal (NP) radium during military service.

## Readjustment Counseling Services

VA provides readjustment counseling services through 207 community-based Vet Centers located in all 50 states, the District of Columbia, Guam, Puerto Rico, and the U.S. Virgin Islands. Counseling is designed to help combat veterans readjust to civilian life.

**Eligibility:** Veterans are eligible if they served on active duty in a combat theater during World War II, the Korean War, the Vietnam War, the Gulf War, or the campaigns in Lebanon, Grenada, Panama, Somalia, Bosnia, Kosovo, Afghanistan, Iraq and the Global War on Terror. Veterans who served in the active military during the Vietnam Era, but not in the Republic of Vietnam, must have requested services at a Vet Center before Jan. 1, 2004.

**Services Offered:** Vet Center staff provide individual, group, family, military sexual trauma, and bereavement counseling. Services include treatment for post-traumatic stress disorder (PTSD) or help with any other military related issue that affects functioning within the family, work, school or other areas of everyday life.   Other services include outreach, education, medical referral, homeless veteran services, employment, VA benefit referral, and the brokering of non-VA services.

**Bereavement Counseling:** Bereavement counseling is available to all family members including spouses, children, parents and siblings of servicemembers who die while on active duty. This includes federally activated members of the National Guard and reserve components. Bereavement services may be accessed by calling (202) 273-9116 or e-mail vet.center@va.gov/.

For additional information, contact the nearest Vet Center, listed in the back of this book, or visit http://www.vetcenter.va.gov/.

# Obtaining Prosthetic and Sensory Aids

Veterans receiving VA care for any condition may receive VA prosthetic appliances, equipment and services, such as home respiratory therapy, artificial limbs, orthopedic braces and therapeutic shoes, wheelchairs, powered mobility, crutches, canes, walkers, and other durable medical equipment and supplies.

VA will provide hearing aids and eyeglasses to veterans who receive increased pension based on the need for regular aid and attendance or being permanently housebound, receive compensation for a service-connected disability or are former POWs. Otherwise, hearing aids and eyeglasses are provided only in special circumstances, and not for normally occurring hearing or vision loss. For additional information, contact the prosthetic representative at the nearest VA health care facility.

# Home Improvements and Structural Alterations for Disability Access

VA provides up to $4,100 for service-connected veterans and up to $1,200 for non service-connected veterans to make home improvements necessary for the continuation of treatment or for disability access to the home and essential lavatory and sanitary facilities. For application information, contact the prosthetic representative at the nearest VA health care facility.

# Services for Blind Veterans

Blind veterans may be eligible for services at a VA medical center or for admission to a VA blind rehabilitation center. In addition, blind veterans enrolled in the VA health care system may receive:

1. A total health and benefits review.
2. Adjustment to blindness training.
3. Home improvements and structural alterations.
4. Specially adapted housing and adaptations.
5. Automobile grant.
6. Low-vision aids and training in their use.
7. Electronic and mechanical aids for the blind, including adaptive computers and computer-assisted devices such as reading machines and electronic travel aids.
8. Guide dogs, including cost of training the veteran to use the dog.
9. Talking books, tapes and Braille literature.

# Mental Health Care Treatment

Veterans eligible for VA medical care may apply for general mental health treatment including specialty services such as PTSD and substance abuse treatment. Contact the nearest VA health care facility to apply.

# Work Restoration Programs

VA provides vocational assistance and therapeutic work opportunities through several programs for veterans receiving VA health care. Each program offers treatment and rehabilitation services to help veterans live and work in their communities.

Participation in the following VA Work Restoration Programs cannot be used to deny or discontinue VA compensation or pension benefits.

**Incentive Therapy:** is a pre-vocational program available at 70 VA Medical Centers and frequently serves as a mainstay for seriously disabled veterans for whom employment is not considered viable in the foreseeable future. Participants receive a token payment for services provided.

**Compensated Work Therapy (CWT):** is a vocational program available at 141 VA Medical Centers. Veterans receive an individualized vocational assessment, rehabilitation planning and work experience with the goal of job placement in the community. The program works closely with community-based organizations, employers and state and federal agencies to establish transitional work experiences, supported employment opportunities, direct job placement and supportive follow-up services.

**CWT/Transitional Residence:** provides work-based, residential treatment in a stable living environment. This program differs from other VA residential bed programs in that participants use their earnings to contribute to the cost of their residences and are responsible for planning, purchasing and preparing their own meals. The program offers a comprehensive array of rehabilitation services including home, financial and life skills management.

# Domiciliary Care Provides Rehabilitative and Long-Term Care to Veterans

Domiciliary care provides rehabilitative and long-term, health-maintenance care for veterans who require minimal medical care but do not need the skilled nursing services provided in nursing homes. A Domiciliary also provides rehabilitative care for veterans who are homeless.

**Eligibility:** VA may provide domiciliary care to veterans whose annual gross household income does not exceed the maximum annual rate of VA pension or to veterans the Secretary of Veterans Affairs determines have no adequate means of support. The co-payments for extended care services apply to domiciliary care. Call your nearest benefits or health care facility to obtain the latest information.

# Outpatient Dental Treatment

VA outpatient dental treatment includes the full spectrum of diagnostic, surgical, restorative and preventive procedures.

**Eligibility:** The following veterans are eligible to receive dental care:

1. Veterans with service-connected, compensable dental conditions.
2. Former POWs.
3. Veterans with service-connected, non-compensable dental conditions as a result of combat wounds or service injuries.
4. Veterans with non service-connected dental conditions determined by VA to be aggravating a service-connected medical problem.
5. Veterans with service-connected conditions rated permanently and totally disabling or 100 percent by reason of un-employability.
6. Veterans in a VA vocational rehabilitation program.
7. Certain enrolled homeless veterans.
8. Veterans with non service-connected dental conditions who received dental treatment while an inpatient in a VA facility.
9. Veterans requiring treatment for dental conditions clinically determined to be complicating a medical condition currently under treatment.

Recently discharged veterans who served on active duty 90 days or more and who apply for VA dental care within 90 days of separation from active duty, may receive a one time dental treatment if their certificate of discharge does not indicate that they received necessary dental care within the 90-day period prior to discharge.

# Outpatient Pharmacy Services

**Eligibility:** VA provides free outpatient pharmacy services to:

1. Veterans with a service-connected disability of 50 percent or more.
2. Veterans receiving medication for service-connected conditions.
3. Veterans whose annual income does not exceed the maximum annual rate of the VA pension.
4. Veterans enrolled in Priority Group 6 who receive medication for service-connected conditions.
5. Veterans receiving medication for conditions related to sexual trauma while serving on active duty.
6. Certain veterans receiving medication for treatment of cancer of the head or neck.
7. Veterans receiving medication for a VA-approved research project.
8. Former POWs.

**Medication Co-pays:** Other veterans will be charged a co-pay of $8 for each 30-day or less supply of medication. For veterans enrolled in Priority Groups 2 through 6, the maximum co-pay amount for calendar year 2007 is $960.

Co-pays apply to prescription and over-the-counter medications, such as aspirin, cough syrup or vitamins, dispensed by a VA pharmacy. However, veterans may prefer to purchase over-the-counter drugs, such as aspirin or vitamins, at a local pharmacy rather than making the co-pay.  Co-pays are not charged for medications injected during the course of treatment or for medical supplies, such as syringes or alcohol wipes.

# Nursing Home Care

The Veterans Health Administration (VHA) provides nursing home services to veterans through three national programs:  VA owned and operated nursing homes, state veterans' homes owned and operated by the states, and the community nursing home program. Each program has admission and eligibility criteria specific to the program.

**VA Nursing Homes:** VA owned and operated nursing homes typically admit residents requiring short-term skilled care or those who have a 70 percent or greater service-connected disability.

**State Veterans' Home Program:** The state veterans' home program is a cooperative venture between the states and VA whereby the states petition VA for matching construction grants and once granted, the state, the veteran, and VA pay a portion of the per diem. The per diem is set in legislation. State veterans homes accept all veterans in need of long-term or short-term nursing home care. Specialized services offered are dependent upon the capability of the home to render them.

**Community Nursing Home Program:** VA maintains contracts with community nursing homes though every VA medical center. The purpose of this program is to meet the nursing home needs of veterans who require long-term nursing home care in their own community, close to their families.

**Eligibility:** The general admission criteria for nursing home placement requires that a resident must be medically stable, i.e. not acutely ill, have sufficient functional deficits to require inpatient nursing home care, and is assessed by an appropriate medical provider to be in need of institutional nursing home care. Furthermore, the veteran must meet the required VA eligibility criteria for nursing home care or the contract nursing home program and the eligibility criteria for the specific state veterans home. For VA nursing home care, a veteran may be subject to a co-payment determined by information supplied by completing a VA Form 10-10EZ. VA social workers are available to assist veterans in interpreting their eligibility and co-pay requirements if indicated.

**Long-Term Care Services:** In addition to nursing home care, VA offers a variety of other long-term care services either directly or by contract with community-based agencies. Such services include adult day health care, inpatient or outpatient respite care, inpatient or outpatient geriatric evaluation and management, hospice and palliative care, and home based primary care. Veterans receiving these services may be subject to a co-pay.

# Emergency Medical Care in Non-VA Facilities

VA may reimburse or pay for medical care provided to enrolled veterans by non-VA facilities only in cases of medical emergencies where VA or other federal facilities were not feasibly available. Other conditions also apply. To determine eligibility or initiate a claim, contact the VA medical facility nearest to where the emergency service was provided.

# National Rehabilitation Special Events

VA sponsors a number of special events as part of recreation therapy provided to veterans under VA care. For information on eligibility and participation, or to be a volunteer, contact the VA National Advisor at the phone number listed below or visit the website at http://www.va.gov/opa/speceven/index.asp.

The schedule for 2007 is as follows:

**Winter Sports Clinic:**  April 1-6, Snowmass, Colo.
Sandy Trombetta (970) 244-1314

**Wheelchair Games:**  June 19-23, Milwaukee, Wis.
Tom Brown (210) 617-5159

**Golden Age Games:**  Aug. 27-31, Houston, Texas
Dewayne Vaughn (202) 745-8615

**Creative Arts Festival:** Oct. 22-28, St. Louis, Mo.
Elizabeth Mackey (320) 255-6351

# *Chapter 2*

# Veterans with Service-Connected Disabilities

*Disability Compensation, Presumptive Conditions for Disability, Programs for Veterans with Service-Connected Disabilities, Vocational Rehabilitation and Employment, Concurrent Retirement and Disability Payments, Combat-Related Special Compensation*

## Disability Compensation

Disability compensation is a monetary benefit paid to veterans who are disabled by an injury or disease that was incurred or aggravated during active military service. These disabilities are considered to be service-connected. Disability compensation varies with the degree of disability and the number of veteran's dependents, and is paid monthly. Veterans with certain severe disabilities may be eligible for additional special monthly compensation.  The benefits are not subject to federal or state income tax.

The payment of military retirement pay, disability severance pay and separation incentive payments known as SSB (Special Separation Benefits) and VSI (Voluntary Separation Incentives) affects the amount of VA compensation paid to disabled veterans.

To be eligible, the service of the veteran must have been terminated through separation or discharge under conditions other than dishonorable. For additional details, visit the website at http://www.vba.va.gov/bln/21/.

| 2007 VA Disability Compensation Rates for Veterans | |
| --- | --- |
| **Veteran's Disability Rating** | **Monthly Rate Paid to Veterans** |
| 10 percent | $115 |
| 20 percent | $225 |
| 30 percent* | $348 |
| 40 percent* | $501 |
| 50 percent* | $712 |
| 60 percent* | $901 |
| 70 percent* | $1,135 |
| 80 percent* | $1,319 |
| 90 percent* | $1,483 |
| 100 percent* | $2,471 |

*Veterans with disability ratings of at least 30 percent are eligible for additional allowances for dependents, including spouses, minor children, children between the ages of 18 and 23 who are attending school, children who are permanently incapable of self-support because of a disability arising before age 18, and dependent parents. The additional amount depends on the disability rating.*

## VA Offers Three Payment Options to Veterans Eligible to Receive Disability Benefits

VA offers three payment options to veterans eligible to receive benefit payments. Most veterans receive their payments by direct deposit to a bank, savings and loan or credit union account. In some areas, veterans who do not have a bank account can open a federally insured Electronic Transfer Account, which costs about $3 a month, provides a monthly statement and allows cash withdrawals. Other veterans may choose to receive benefits by check. To choose a payment method, call toll-free 1-877-838-2778, Monday through Friday, 7:30 a.m. - 4 p.m., CST.

## Presumptive Conditions Considered for Awarding Disability Compensation

Certain veterans are eligible for disability compensation based on the presumption that their disability is service connected.

**Prisoners of War:** For former POWs who were imprisoned for any length of time, the following disabilities are presumed to be service-connected if they are rated at least 10 percent disabling anytime after military service: psychosis, any of the anxiety states, dysthymic disorder, organic residuals of frostbite, post-traumatic osteoarthritis, heart disease or hypertensive vascular disease and their complications, stroke and residuals of stroke.

For former POWs who were imprisoned for at least 30 days, the following conditions are also presumed to be service-connected: avitaminosis, beriberi, chronic dysentery, helminthiasis, malnutrition (including optic atrophy), pellagra and/or other nutritional deficiencies, irritable bowel syndrome, peptic ulcer disease, peripheral neuropathy and cirrhosis of the liver.

**Veterans Exposed to Agent Orange and Other Herbicides:** A veteran who served in the Republic of Vietnam between Jan. 9, 1962, and May 7, 1975, is presumed to have been exposed to Agent Orange and other herbicides used in support of military operations.

Eleven diseases are presumed by VA to be service-connected for such veterans: chloracne or other acneform disease similar to chloracne, porphyria cutanea tarda, soft-tissue sarcoma (other than osteosarcoma, chondrosarcoma, Kaposi's sarcoma or mesothelioma), Hodgkin's disease, multiple myeloma, respiratory cancers (lung, bronchus, larynx, trachea), non-Hodgkin's lymphoma, prostate cancer, acute and subacute peripheral neuropathy, diabetes mellitus (Type 2) and chronic lymphocytic leukemia.

**Veterans Exposed to Radiation:** For veterans who participated in "radiation risk activities" as defined in VA regulations while on active duty, the following conditions are presumed to be service-connected: all forms of leukemia (except for chronic lymphocytic leukemia); cancer of the thyroid, breast, pharynx, esophagus, stomach, small intestine, pancreas, bile ducts, gall bladder, salivary gland, urinary tract (renal pelvis, ureter, urinary bladder and urethra), brain, bone, lung, colon, and ovary, bronchiolo-alveolar carcinoma, multiple myeloma, lymphomas (other than Hodgkin's disease), and primary liver cancer (except if cirrhosis or hepatitis B is indicated).

To determine service-connection for other conditions or exposures not eligible for presumptive service-connection, VA considers factors such as the amount of radiation exposure, duration of exposure, elapsed time between exposure and onset of the disease, gender and family history, age at time of exposure, the extent to which a non service-related exposure could contribute to disease, and the relative sensitivity of exposed tissue.

## Gulf War Veterans May Receive Disability Compensation for Chronic Disabilities

Gulf War veterans may receive disability compensation for chronic disabilities resulting from undiagnosed illnesses, medically unexplained chronic multi-symptom illnesses defined by a cluster of signs or symptoms.  A disability is considered chronic if it has existed for at least six months.  The undiagnosed illnesses must have appeared either during active service in the Southwest Asia Theater of Operations during the Gulf War or to a degree of at least 10 percent at any time since then through Dec. 31, 2011.

The following are examples of symptoms of an undiagnosed illness: chronic fatigue syndrome, fibromyalgia, skin disorders, headache, muscle pain, joint pain, neurological symptoms, neuropsychological symptoms, symptoms involving the respiratory system, sleep disturbances, gastrointestinal symptoms, cardiovascular symptoms, abnormal weight loss, and menstrual disorders.

Amyotrophic Lateral Sclerosis (ALS), also known as Lou Gehrig's Disease, may be determined to be service-connected if the veteran served in the Southwest Asia Theater of Operations anytime during the period of Aug. 2, 1990, to July 31, 1991. The Southwest Asia Theater of Operations includes Iraq, Kuwait, Saudi Arabia, the neutral zone between Iraq and Saudi Arabia, Bahrain, Qatar, the United Arab Emirates, Oman, the Gulf of Aden, the Gulf of Oman, the Persian Gulf, the Arabian Sea, the Red Sea, and the airspace above these locations.

# Programs for Veterans with Service-Connected Disabilities

## Vocational Rehabilitation and Employment

The Vocational Rehabilitation and Employment Program assists veterans who have service-connected disabilities with obtaining and maintaining suitable employment. Independent living services are also available for severely disabled veterans who are not currently ready to seek employment. Additional information is available on the website at http://www.vba.va.gov/bln/vre/.

**Eligibility:** A veteran must have a VA service-connected disability rated at least 20 percent with an employment handicap, or rated 10 percent with a serious employment handicap, and be discharged or released from military service under other than dishonorable conditions. Servicemembers pending medical separation from active duty may also apply if their disabilities are reasonably expected to be rated at least 20 percent following their discharge.

**Services:** VA pays the cost of all approved training programs. Subsistence allowance may also be provided.  Depending on an individual's needs, services provided by VA may include:

1. An evaluation of interests, aptitudes and abilities.
2. Assistance with writing a resume and other job seeking skills.
3. Assistance with obtaining and maintaining suitable employment.
4. Vocational counseling and planning.
5. On-the-job training and work-experience programs.
6. Training, such as certificate, two, or four-year college or technical programs.
7. Supportive rehabilitation services and counseling.

**Period of a Rehabilitation Program:** Generally, veterans must complete a program within 12 years from their separation from military service or within 12 years from the date VA notifies them that they have a compensable service-connected disability. Depending on the length of program needed, veterans may be provided up to 48 months of full-time services or their part-time equivalent. These limitations may be extended in certain circumstances.

**Work-Study:** Veterans training at the three-quarter or full-time rate may participate in VA's work-study program. Participants may provide VA outreach services, prepare and process VA paperwork, and work at a VA medical facility or perform other VA-approved activities. A portion of the work-study allowance equal to 40 percent of the total may be paid in advance.

# Fiscal Year 2007 VA Vocational Rehabilitation Monthly Payment Rate Schedules

For institutional or independent living training, or unpaid work experience in a federal, state, or local agency, or an agency of a federally recognized Indian tribe, the rates are:

| Training Time | Veterans With No Dependents | Veterans With One Dependent | Veterans With Two Dependents | Each Additional Dependent |
|---|---|---|---|---|
| Full-time | $508.04 | $630.19 | $742.61 | $54.14 |
| 3/4-time | $381.73 | $473.32 | $555.21 | $41.63 |
| 1/2-time | $255.42 | $316.47 | $372.00 | $27.78 |

For unpaid on-the-job training in federal, state, or local agency, or an agency of a federally recognized Indian tribe; training in a home; vocational course in a rehabilitation facility or sheltered workshop; independent instructor; institutional non-farm cooperative, the rates are:

| Training Time | Veterans With No Dependents | Veterans With One Dependent | Veterans With Two Dependents | Each Additional Dependent |
|---|---|---|---|---|
| Full-time | $508.04 | $630.19 | $742.61 | $54.14 |

For farm cooperative, apprenticeship, on-the-job training, or on-the-job non-farm cooperative, VA payments are variable, based on the wages received.  The maximum VA rates are:

| Training Time | Veterans With No Dependents | Veterans With One Dependent | Veterans With Two Dependents | Each Additional Dependent |
|---|---|---|---|---|
| Full-time | $444.19 | $537.16 | $619.07 | $40.27 |

For extended evaluation, the rates are:

| Training Time | Veterans With No Dependents | Veterans With One Dependent | Veterans With Two Dependents | Each Additional Dependent |
|---|---|---|---|---|
| Full-time | $508.04 | $630.19 | $742.61 | $54.14 |
| 3/4-time | $381.73 | $473.32 | $555.21 | $41.63 |
| 1/2-time | $255.42 | $316.47 | $372.00 | $27.78 |
| 1/4–time | $127.70 | $158.24 | $185.99 | $13.85 |

## Some Veterans May be Entitled to Specially Adapted Housing (SAH) Grants from VA

Certain veterans and servicemembers with service-connected disabilities may be entitled to a Specially Adapted Housing (SAH) grant from VA to help build a new specially adapted house or buy a house and modify it to meet their disability-related requirements. Eligible veterans or servicemembers may now receive up to three grants, with the total dollar amount of the grants not to exceed the maximum allowable.  Previous grant recipients who had received assistance of less than the current maximum allowable may be eligible for an additional SAH grant.

Eligible veterans who are temporarily residing in a home owned by a family member may also receive assistance in the form of a grant to assist the veteran in adapting the family member's home to meet his or her special needs.  Those eligible for a $50,000 total grant would be permitted to use up to $14,000 and those eligible for a $10,000 total grant would be permitted to use up to $2,000. (See eligibility requirements for different grant amounts.) However, VA is not authorized to make such grants available to assist active duty personnel.

**Eligibility for up to $50,000:** VA may approve a grant of not more than 50 percent of the cost of building, buying, or adapting existing homes or paying to reduce indebtedness on a previously owned home that is being adapted, up to a maximum of $50,000. In certain instances, the full grant amount may be applied toward remodeling costs. Veterans and servicemembers must be determined eligible to receive compensation for permanent and total service-connected disability due to one of the following:

1. Loss or loss of use of both lower extremities, such as to preclude locomotion without the aid of braces, crutches, canes or a wheelchair.
2. Loss or loss of use of both upper extremities at or above the elbow.
3. Blindness in both eyes, having only light perception, plus loss or loss of use of one lower extremity.
4. Loss or loss of use of one lower extremity together with (a) residuals of organic disease or injury, or (b) the loss or loss of use of one upper extremity which so affects the functions of balance or propulsion as to preclude locomotion without the use of braces, canes, crutches or a wheelchair.

**Eligibility for up to $10,000:** VA may approve a grant for the cost, up to a maximum of $10,000, for necessary adaptations to a veteran's or servicemember's residence or to help veterans and servicemembers acquire a residence already adapted with special features for their disability. To be eligible for this grant, veterans and servicemembers must be entitled to compensation for permanent and total service-connected disability due to:

1. Blindness in both eyes with 5/200 visual acuity or less.
2. Or anatomical loss or loss of use of both hands.

**Supplemental Financing:** Veterans and servicemembers with available loan guaranty entitlement may also obtain a guaranteed loan or a direct loan from VA to supplement the grant to acquire a specially adapted home. Amounts with a guaranteed loan from a private lender will vary, but the maximum direct loan from VA is $33,000.

# Veterans Requiring Assistance with Adapting an Automobile to Meet Disability Needs

Veterans and servicemembers may be eligible for a one-time payment of not more than $11,000 toward the purchase of an automobile or other conveyance if they have service-connected loss or permanent loss of use of one or both hands or feet, permanent impairment of vision of both eyes to a certain degree, or ankylosis (immobility) of one or both knees or one or both hips.

They may also be eligible for adaptive equipment, and for repair, replacement, or reinstallation required because of disability or for the safe operation of a vehicle purchased with VA assistance. To apply, contact a VA regional office at 1-800-827-1000 or the nearest VA medical center.

# Annual Clothing Allowance for Veterans With Service-Connected Disabilities

Any veteran who is service-connected for a disability for which he or she uses prosthetic or orthopedic appliances may receive an annual clothing allowance.

The clothing allowance also is available to any veteran whose service-connected skin condition requires prescribed medication that irreparably damages his or her outer garments. To apply, contact the prosthetic representative at the nearest VA medical center.

# Veterans Requiring Aid and Attendance or Housebound Veterans

A veteran who is determined by VA to be in need of the regular aid and attendance of another person, or a veteran who is permanently housebound, may be entitled to additional disability compensation or pension payments. A veteran evaluated at 30 percent or more disabled is entitled to receive an additional payment for a spouse who is in need of the aid and attendance of another person.

# Concurrent Retirement and Disability Payments (CRDP) for Disabled Veterans

Concurrent Retirement and Disability Payments (CRDP) restores retired pay on a graduated 10-year schedule for retirees with a 50 to 90 percent VA-rated disability.  Concurrent retirement payments increase 10 percent per year through 2013.  Veterans rated 100% disabled by VA are entitled to full CRDP without being phased in.  Veterans receiving benefits at the 100% rate due to individual unemployability are entitled to full CRDP in 2009.

**Eligibility:** To qualify, veterans must also meet all three of the following criteria:

1. Have 20 or more years on active duty, or a reservist age 60 or older with 20 or more creditable years.
2. Be in a retired status.
3. Be receiving retired pay (must be offset by VA payments).

Retirees do not need to apply for this benefit.  Payment is coordinated between VA and the Department of Defense (DOD).

# Combat-Related Special Compensation (CRSC) for Retired Veterans

Combat-Related Special Compensation (CRSC) provides tax-free monthly payments to eligible retired veterans with combat-related injuries.  With CRSC, veterans can receive both their full military retirement pay and their VA disability compensation, if the injury is combat-related.

**Eligibility:** Retired veterans with combat-related injuries must meet all of the following criteria to apply for CRSC:

1. Active, Reserve, or medically retired with 20 years of creditable service.
2. Receiving military retired pay.
3. Have a 10% or greater VA-rated injury.
4. Military retired pay is reduced by VA disability payments (VA Waiver).

In addition, veterans must be able to provide documentary evidence that their injuries were a result of one of the following:

- Training that simulates war (e.g., exercises, field training)
- Hazardous duty (e.g., flight, diving, parachute duty)
- An instrumentality of war (e.g. combat vehicles, weapons, Agent Orange)
- Armed conflict (e.g. gunshot wounds {Purple Heart}, punji stick injuries)

For more information, visit the website at http://www.dod.mil/prhome/mppcrsc.html, or call the toll free phone number for the veteran's branch of service:  (Army) 1-866-281-3254; (Air Force) 1-800-616-3775; (Navy) 1-877-366-2772; and (Coast Guard) 1-866-307-1336.

# *Chapter 3*

# VA Pensions

*Eligibility for Disability Pension, Improved Disability Pension,
Payment Rates, Protected Pension Programs,
Medal of Honor Pension*

## Eligibility for Disability Pension

Veterans with low incomes who are permanently and totally disabled, or are age 65 and older, may be eligible for monetary support if they have 90 days or more of active military service, at least one day of which was during a period of war. (Veterans who entered active duty on or after Sept. 8, 1980, or officers who entered active duty on or after Oct. 16, 1981, may have to meet a longer minimum period of active duty). The veteran's discharge must have been under conditions other than dishonorable and the disability must be for reasons other than the veteran's own willful misconduct.

Payments are made to bring the veteran's total income, including other retirement or Social Security income, to a level set by Congress. Un-reimbursed medical expenses may reduce countable income for VA purposes.

## Improved Disability Pension

Congress establishes the maximum annual improved disability pension rates. Payments are reduced by the amount of countable income of the veteran, spouse or dependent children. When a veteran without a spouse or a child is furnished nursing home or domiciliary care by VA, the pension is reduced to an amount not to exceed $90 per month after three calendar months of care. The reduction may be delayed if nursing-home care is being continued to provide the veteran with rehabilitation services.

| 2007 VA Improved Disability Pension Rates | |
| --- | --- |
| **Status of Veteran's Family Situation and Caretaking Needs** | **Maximum Annual Rate** |
| Veteran without dependents | $10,929 |
| Veteran with one dependent | $14,313 |
| Veteran permanently housebound, no dependents | $13,356 |
| Veteran permanently housebound, one dependent | $16,740 |
| Veteran needing regular aid and attendance, no dependents | $18,243 |
| Veteran needing regular aid and attendance, one dependent | $21,615 |
| Two veterans married to one another | $14,313 |
| Increase for each additional dependent child | $1,866 |

*Additional information can be found in the Compensation and Pension Benefits section of VA's Internet pages at http://www. vba.va.gov/bln/21/index.htm.*

# Protected Pension Programs

Pension beneficiaries who were receiving a VA pension on Dec. 31, 1978, and do not wish to elect the Improved Pension will continue to receive the pension rate they were receiving on that date. This rate generally continues as long as the beneficiary's income remains within established limits, his or her net worth does not bar payment, and the beneficiary does not lose any dependents.

These beneficiaries must continue to meet basic eligibility factors, such as permanent and total disability for veterans, or status as a surviving spouse or child. VA must adjust rates for other reasons, such as a veteran's hospitalization in a VA facility.

# Medal of Honor Pension

VA administers pensions to recipients of the Medal of Honor. Congress set the monthly pension at $1,104 effective Dec. 1, 2006.

# *Chapter 4*

# Education and Training

*Montgomery GI Bill, Types of Training Available,
Work-Study Program, Educational and Vocational Counseling,
Veterans' Educational Assistance Program*

This chapter provides a summary of VA educational and training benefits. Additional information can be found at http://www.gibill.va.gov/ or by calling 1-888-GI-BILL-1 (1-888-442-4551).

## Montgomery GI Bill (MGIB)

**Eligibility:** VA educational benefits may be used while the servicemember is on active duty or after the servicemember's separation from active duty with a fully honorable military discharge. Discharges "under honorable conditions" and "general" discharges do not establish eligibility.

Eligibility generally expires 10 years after the servicemember's discharge. However, there are exceptions for disability, re-entering active duty, and upgraded discharges.

All participants must have a high school diploma, equivalency certificate, or completed 12 hours toward a college degree before applying for benefits.

Previously, servicemembers had to meet the high school requirement before they completed their initial active duty obligation. Those who did not may now meet the requirement and reapply for benefits. If eligible, they must use their benefits either within 10 years from the date of last discharge from active duty or by Nov. 2, 2010, whichever is later.

Additionally, every veteran must establish eligibility under one of four categories.

# Category 1 – Service after June 30, 1985

For veterans who entered active duty for the first time after June 30, 1985, did not decline MGIB in writing, and had their military pay reduced by $100 a month for 12 months.

Servicemembers can apply after completing two continuous years of service. Veterans must have completed three continuous years of active duty, or two continuous years of active duty if they first signed up for less than three years or have an obligation to serve four years in the Selected Reserve (the 2x4 program) and enter the Selected Reserve within one year of discharge.

Servicemembers or veterans who received a commission as a result of graduation from a service academy or completion of an ROTC scholarship are not eligible under Category 1 unless they received their commission:

1. After becoming eligible for MGIB benefits (including completing the minimum service requirements for the initial period of active duty).
2. Or after Sept. 30, 1996, and received less than $3,400 during any one year under ROTC scholarship.

Servicemembers or veterans who declined MGIB because they received repayment from the military for education loans are also ineligible under Category 1. If they did not decline MGIB and re-ceived loan repayments, the months served to repay the loans will be deducted from their entitlement.

**Early Separation from Military Service:** Servicemembers who did not complete the required period of military service may be eligible under Category 1 if discharged for one of the following:

1. Convenience of the government—with 30 continuous

    months of service for an obligation of three or more years,
or 20 continuous months of service for an obligation of less
than three years.
2. Service-connected disability.
3. Hardship.
4. A medical condition diagnosed prior to joining the military.
5. A condition that interfered with performance of duty and did
not result from misconduct.
6. A reduction in force (in most cases).

# Category 2 – Vietnam Era GI Bill Conversion

For veterans who had remaining entitlement under the Vietnam Era
GI Bill on Dec. 31, 1989, and served on active duty for any number
of days during the period Oct. 19, 1984, to June 30, 1985, for at least
three continuous years beginning on July 1, 1985; or at least two
continuous years of active duty beginning on July 1, 1985, followed
by four years in the Selected Reserve beginning within one year of
release from active duty.

Veterans not on active duty on Oct. 19, 1984, may be eligible under Category 2 if they served three continuous years on active duty
beginning on or after July 1, 1985, or two continuous years of active
duty at any time followed by four continuous years in the Selected
Reserve beginning within one year of release from active duty.

Veterans are barred from eligibility under Category 2 if they received
a commission after Dec. 31, 1976, as a result of graduation from a
service academy or completion of an ROTC scholarship.

However, such a commission is not a bar if they received the commission after becoming eligible for MGIB benefits, or received the
commission after Sept. 30, 1996, and received less than $3,400 dur-
ing any one year under ROTC scholarship.

# Category 3 – Involuntary Separation/Special Separation

For veterans who meet one of the following requirements:
    1. Elected MGIB before being involuntarily separated.

2.  Or were voluntarily separated under the Voluntary Separation Incentive or the Special Separation Benefit program, elected MGIB benefits before being separated, and had military pay reduced by $1,200 before discharge.

# Category 4 – Veterans Educational Assistance Program (VEAP)

For veterans who participated in the Veterans Educational Assistance Program (VEAP) and:

1. Served on active duty on Oct. 9, 1996.
2. Participated in VEAP and contributed money to an account.
3. Elected MGIB by Oct. 9, 1997, and paid $1,200.

Veterans who participated in VEAP on or before Oct. 9, 1996, may also be eligible even if they did not deposit money in a VEAP account if they served on active duty from Oct. 9, 1996, through April 1, 2000, elected MGIB by Oct. 31, 2001, and contributed $2,700 to MGIB.

Certain National Guard servicemembers may also qualify under Category 4 if they:

1. Served for the first time on full-time active duty in the National Guard between June 30, 1985, and Nov. 29, 1989, and had no previous active duty service.
2. Elected MGIB during the nine-month window ending on July 9, 1997.
3. And paid $1,200.

**Payments:** Effective Oct. 1, 2006, the rate for full-time training in college, technical or vocational school is $1,075 a month for those who served three years or more or two years plus four years in the Selected Reserve. For those who served less than three years, the monthly rate is $873. Benefits are reduced for part-time training. Payments for other types of training follow different rules. VA will pay an additional amount, called a "kicker" or "college fund," if directed by DOD.  Visit www.gibill.va.gov/ for more information.
The maximum number of months veterans can receive payments is 36 months at the full-time rate or the part-time equivalent.

The following groups qualify for the maximum: veterans who served the required length of active duty, veterans with an obligation of three years or more who were separated early for the convenience of the government and served 30 continuous months, and veterans with an obligation of less than three years who were separated early for the convenience of the government and served 20 continuous months.

**Types of Training Available:** The following types of training are available:

1. Courses at colleges and universities leading to associate, bachelor or graduate degrees, including accredited independent study offered through distance education.
2. Courses leading to a certificate or diploma from business, technical or vocational schools.
3. Apprenticeship or on-the-job training for those not on active duty, including self-employment training begun on or after June 16, 2004, for ownership or operation of a franchise.
4. Correspondence courses, under certain conditions.
5. Flight training, if the veteran holds a private pilot's license upon beginning the training program and meets the medical requirements.
6. State-approved teacher certification programs.
7. Preparatory courses necessary for admission to a college or graduate school.
8. License and certification tests approved for veterans.
9. Entrepreneurship training courses to create or expand small businesses.
10. Tuition assistance using MGIB as "Top-Up" (active duty servicemembers).

**Work-Study Program:** Veterans who train at the three-quarter or full-time rate may be eligible for a work-study program in which they work for VA and receive hourly wages. The types of work allowed include:

1. Outreach services.
2. VA paperwork.
3. Work at national or state veterans' cemeteries.
4. Work at VA medical centers or state veterans' homes.
5. Other VA approved activities.

**Educational and Vocational Counseling:** VA counseling is available to help determine educational or vocational strengths and weaknesses and plan educational or employment goals.

Additionally, individuals not eligible for the MGIB may still receive VA counseling beginning 180 days prior to separation from active duty through the first full year following honorable discharge.

# Eligibility for Veterans' Educational Assistance Program (VEAP)

**Eligibility:** Active duty personnel could participate in the Veterans' Educational Assistance Program (VEAP) if they entered active duty for the first time after Dec. 31, 1976, and before July 1, 1985, and made a contribution prior to April 1, 1987. The maximum contribution is $2,700. Active duty participants may make a lump-sum contribution to their VEAP account.  For more information, visit the webite at www.gibill.va.gov/.

Servicemembers who participated in VEAP are eligible to receive benefits while on active duty if:

1.  At least three months of contributions are available, except for high school or elementary, in which only one month is needed.
2.  And they enlisted for the first time after Sept. 7, 1980, and completed 24 months of their first period of active duty.

Servicemembers must receive a discharge under conditions other than dishonorable for the qualifying period of service. Servicemembers who enlisted for the first time after Sept. 7, 1980, or entered active duty as an officer or enlistee after Oct. 16, 1981, must have completed 24 continuous months of active duty, unless they meet a qualifying exception.

Eligibility generally expires 10 years from release from active duty, but can be extended under special circumstances.

**Payments:** DOD will match contributions at the rate of $2 for every $1 put into the fund and may make additional contributions, or "kickers," as necessary. For training in college, vocational or technical schools, the payment amount depends on the type and hours of training pursued. The maximum amount is $300 a month for full-time training.

**Training, Work-Study, Counseling:** VEAP participants may receive the same training, work-study benefits and counseling as provided under the Montgomery GI Bill.

# *Chapter 5*

# Home Loan Guaranty

*VA Loan Uses, Eligibility, Guaranty Amount Varies with Size of Loan, VA Appraisals Required Before Loans are Guaranteed by VA, Financing, Loan Assumption Requirements and Liability, Loans for Native American Veterans, Safeguards Established to Protect Veterans*

VA home loan guaranties are issued to help eligible servicemembers, veterans, reservists and unmarried surviving spouses obtain homes, condominiums, residential cooperative housing units, and manufactured homes, and to refinance loans. For additional information or to obtain VA loan guaranty forms, visit http://www.homeloans.va.gov/.

**Loan Uses:** A VA guaranty helps protect lenders from loss if the borrower fails to repay the loan. It can be used to obtain a loan to:

1. Buy or build a home.
2. Buy a residential condominium.
3. Buy a residential cooperative housing unit.
4. Repair, alter or improve a home.
5. Refinance an existing home loan.
6. Buy a manufactured home with or without a lot.
7. Buy and improve a manufactured home lot.
8. Install a solar heating or cooling system or other weatherization improvements.
9. Buy a home and install energy-efficient improvements.

# Eligibility

In addition to the periods of eligibility and conditions of service requirements, applicants must have a good credit rating, sufficient income, a valid Certificate of Eligibility, and agree to live in the property.

To obtain a Certificate of Eligibility, complete VA Form 26-1880 -- "Request for a Certificate of Eligibility for VA Home Loan" -- and mail to: VA Eligibility Center, P.O. Box 20729, Winston-Salem, NC  27120.

Applicants may also have their lenders obtain a Certificate of Eligibility for them through VA's Automated Certificate of Eligibility (ACE) system. In many cases, ACE can generate an online certificate immediately. However, not all cases can be processed this way. For more information, visit http://www.homeloans.va.gov/eligibility.htm.

# Periods of Eligibility

**World War II:** (1) active duty service after Sept. 15, 1940, and prior to July 26, 1947; (2) discharge under other than dishonorable conditions; and (3) at least 90 days service unless discharged early for a service-connected disability.

**Post-World War II:** (1) active duty service after July 25, 1947, and prior to June 27, 1950; (2) discharge under other than dishonorable conditions; and (3) 181 days continuous active duty service unless discharged early for a service-connected disability.

**Korean War:** (1) active duty after June 26, 1950, and prior to Feb. 1, 1955; (2) discharge under other than dishonorable conditions; and (3) at least 90 days total service, unless discharged early for a service-connected disability.

**Post-Korean War:** (1) active duty between Jan. 31, 1955, and Aug. 5, 1964; (2) discharge under conditions other than dishonorable; (3) 181 days continuous service, unless discharged early for a service-connected disability.

**Vietnam:** (1) active duty after Aug. 4, 1964, and prior to May 8, 1975; (2) discharge under conditions other than dishonorable; and (3) 90 days total service, unless discharged early for a service-connected disability. For veterans who served in the Republic of Vietnam, the beginning date is Feb. 28, 1961.

**Post-Vietnam:** (1) For veterans whose enlisted service began before Sept. 8, 1980, or whose service as an officer began before Oct. 17, 1981; (2) active duty for 181 continuous days, all of which occurred after May 7, 1975; and (3) discharge under conditions other than dishonorable or early discharge for service-connected disability.

**24-Month Rule:** If service was between Sept. 8, 1980, (Oct. 16, 1981, for officers) and Aug. 1, 1990, veterans must generally complete 24 months of continuous active duty service or the full period (at least 181 days) for which they were called or ordered to active duty, and be discharged under conditions other than dishonorable.

Exceptions are allowed if the veteran completed at least 181 days of active duty service but was discharged earlier than 24 months for (1) hardship, (2) the convenience of the government, (3) reduction-in-force, (4) certain medical conditions, or (5) service-connected disability.

**Gulf War:** Veterans of the Gulf War era must generally complete 24 months of continuous active duty service or the full period (at least 90 days) for which they were called to active duty, and be discharged under conditions other than dishonorable.

Exceptions are allowed if the veteran completed at least 90 days of active duty but was discharged earlier than 24 months for (1) hardship, (2) the convenience of the government, (3) reduction-in-force, (4) certain medical conditions, or (5) service-connected disability. Reservists and National Guard members are eligible if they were activated after Aug. 1, 1990, served at least 90 days, and received an honorable discharge.

**Active Duty Personnel:** Until the Gulf War era is ended, persons on active duty are eligible after serving 90 continuous days.

# Guaranty Amount Varies with Size of Loan

The VA guaranty varies with the size of the loan, and is issued to protect lenders so they may make loans to eligible borrowers. Because the lenders are able to obtain this guaranty from VA, borrowers do not need to make a down payment, provided they have enough home loan entitlement.

The maximum guaranty amount is equal to 25 percent of the Freddie Mac conforming loan limit for a single family home. This limit changes yearly, but is set at $417,000 for calendar year 2007 ($625,500 for Hawaii, Alaska, Guam and the U.S. Virgin Islands).

| 2007 VA Home Loan Guaranty Entitlement | | |
|---|---|---|
| Loan Amount | Percentage of Loan Guaranteed | Maximum Guaranty Amount |
| $0.00 - $45,000 | 50% | $22,500 |
| $45,001 - $56,250 | 50% - 40% | $22,500 |
| $56,251 - $144,000 | 40% - 25% | $36,000 |
| $144,001 or more | 25% | $104,250 |
| Manufactured Home or Lot | 40% | $20,000 |

The total loan amount may include the Funding Fee, as well as up to $6,000 of home improvements to make the home more energy efficient.

An eligible borrower who wishes to use a VA-guaranteed loan to refinance an existing mortgage generally can borrow up to 90 percent of the home's appraised value. However, a loan to reduce the interest rate on an existing VA-guaranteed loan may include the entire outstanding balance of the prior loan, the costs of energy-efficient modifications, as well as up to two discount points of loan closing fees. An eligible borrower who wishes to obtain a VA-guaranteed loan to purchase a manufactured home or lot can only borrow up to

95 percent of the home's purchase price.

## VA Appraisals of Properties Required Before Loans are Guaranteed by VA

No loan can be guaranteed by VA without first being appraised by a qualified VA fee appraiser. A buyer, seller, real estate agent or lender can request a VA appraisal by completing VA Form 26-1805, "Request for Determination of Reasonable Value." The requester pays for the appraisal according to a fee schedule approved by VA.

This VA appraisal estimates the value of the property. It is not an inspection and does not guarantee the house is free of defects. VA guarantees the loan, not the condition of the property.

## Payment in Cash is Required on All Closing Costs for VA Loans

Payment in cash is required on all closing costs, including title search and recording fees, hazard insurance premiums and prepaid taxes. For refinancing loans, all such costs may be included in the loan, as long as the total loan does not exceed 90 percent of the reasonable value of the property. Interest rate reduction loans may include closing costs and a maximum of two discount points.

All loans, except those made to disabled veterans and unmarried surviving spouses of veterans who died as a result of service, are charged a VA funding fee. This fee is based on the loan amount and may be included in the loan.

| 2007 VA Funding Fee Schedule Assessed to Veterans and Servicemembers with VA Home Loans | | |
|---|---|---|
| **Loan Category** | **Active Duty Servicemembers and Veterans Pay VA** | **Reservists Pay VA** |
| Purchase or construction loans with down payments of less than 5%, refinancing loans, and home improvement loans. | 2.15% | 2.40% |
| Purchase or construction loans with down payments of at least 5% but less than 10% | 1.50% | 1.75% |
| Purchase or construction loans with down payments of 10% or more | 1.25% | 1.50% |
| Manufactured home loans | 1.00% | 1.00% |
| Interest rate reduction loans | 0.50% | 0.50% |
| Assumption of VA-guaranteed loans | 0.50% | 0.50% |
| Second or subsequent use of entitlement with no down payment | 3.35%* | 3.35%* |

*The funding fee temporarily increased from 3.3% to 3.35% for fiscal year 2007. The funding fee will be 3.3% again beginning Oct. 1, 2007.*

# Required Occupancy

To qualify for a VA guaranty, a veteran or the spouse of a service-member must certify that he or she intends to live in the home. When refinancing a VA-guaranteed loan solely to reduce the interest rate, a veteran need only certify to prior occupancy.

# Financing, Interest Rates and Terms

Veterans obtain VA-guaranteed loans through the usual lending institutions, including banks, savings and loan associations and mortgage brokers. VA-guaranteed loans can have either a fixed interest rate or an adjustable rate, where the interest rate may adjust up to one percent annually and up to five percent over the life of the loan.

Veterans may also choose a different type of adjustable rate mortgage called a hybrid ARM, where the initial interest rate remains fixed for three to 10 years. If the rate remains fixed for less than five years, the rate adjustment cannot be more than one percent annually and five percent over the life of the loan.

For a hybrid ARM with an initial fixed period of five years or more, the initial adjustment may be up to two percent. Adjustments thereafter are limited to one percent annually and six percent over the life of the loan.

If the lender charges discount points on the loan, the veteran may negotiate with the seller as to who will pay points or if they will be split between buyer and seller. Points paid by the veteran may not be included in the loan (with the exception that up to two points may be included in interest rate reduction loans). The loan may be for as long as 30 years and 32 days.

# Loan Assumption Requirements and Liability

VA loans made on or after March 1, 1988, are not assumable without the prior approval of VA or its authorized agent (usually the lender collecting the monthly payments). To approve the assumption, the lender must ensure that the purchaser is a satisfactory credit risk and will assume all of the veteran's liabilities on the loan.

If approved, the purchaser will have to pay a funding fee that the lender sends to VA, and the veteran will be released from liability to the federal government.  A release of liability does not mean that a veteran's guaranty entitlement is restored. That occurs only if the buyer is a veteran and agrees to substitute his or her entitlement for that of the seller.

If a veteran allows assumption of a loan without prior approval, then the lender may demand immediate and full payment of the loan, and the veteran may be liable if the loan is foreclosed and VA has to pay a claim under the loan guaranty.

Loans made prior to March 1, 1988, are generally freely assumable, but veterans should still request VA's approval in order to be released of liability. Veterans whose loans were closed after Dec. 31, 1989, usually have no liability to the government following a foreclosure, except in cases involving fraud, misrepresentation, or bad faith, such as allowing an unapproved assumption.

## VA Acquires Property Foreclosures

VA acquires properties as a result of foreclosures. The properties are marketed by Ocwen Loan Servicing, LLC, through listing agents using local Multiple Listing Services. A listing of "VA Properties for Sale" may be found at http://www.ocwen.com/reo/home.cfm.  Contact a real estate agent for information on purchasing a VA acquired property.

## Loans for Native American Veterans

Eligible Native American veterans can obtain a loan from VA to purchase, construct or improve a home on Federal Trust land, or to reduce the interest rate on such a VA loan. The maximum loan amount is equal to the Freddie Mac conforming loan limit for a single-family home.  This limit changes yearly.  In 2007, the limit is $417,000 for the continental United States and $625,500 for Hawaii, Alaska, and Guam.

Veterans who are not Native American, but who are married to Native American non-veterans, may be eligible for a direct loan under this program.  To be eligible for such a loan, the qualified non-Native

American veteran and the Native American spouse must reside on Federal Trust land, and both the veteran and spouse must have a meaningful interest in the dwelling or lot.

A funding fee must be paid to VA, unless the veteran is exempt from such a fee because they receive either VA disability compensation or military retirement pay. The fee, which is 1.25 percent for loans to purchase, construct or improve a home, and 0.5 percent to refinance an existing loan, may be paid in cash or included in the loan.

The following may not be included in the loan: VA appraisal, credit report, loan processing fee, title search, title insurance, recording fees, transfer taxes, survey charges or hazard insurance.

## Safeguards Established to Protect Veterans

The following safeguards have been established to protect veterans:

1. Homes completed less than a year before purchase with VA financing and inspected during construction by either VA or the Department of Housing and Urban Development (HUD) must meet VA requirements.
2. VA may suspend from the loan program those who take unfair advantage of veterans or discriminate because of race, color, religion, sex, disability, family status or national origin.
3. The builder of a new home (or manufactured home) is required to give the purchasing veteran a one-year warranty that the home has been constructed to VA-approved plans and specifications.
4. In cases of new construction completed under VA or HUD inspection, VA may compensate a veteran borrower for correction of structural defects seriously affecting livability if requested within four years of a home loan guaranty.
5. The borrower obtaining a loan may only be charged the fees and other charges prescribed by VA as allowable.
6. The borrower can prepay without penalty the entire loan or any part not less than one installment or $100.
7. VA encourages holders to extend forbearance if a borrower becomes temporarily unable to meet the terms of the loan.

# Chapter 6

# VA Life Insurance

*Servicemembers' Group Life Insurance, Traumatic Injury Protection Under Servicemembers' Group Life Insurance, Family Servicemembers' Group Life Insurance, Veterans' Group Life Insurance, Service-Disabled Veterans Insurance, Veterans' Mortgage Life Insurance*

For complete details on government life insurance, visit the VA Internet site at http://www.insurance.va.gov/ or call toll-free 1-800-669-8477. Specialists are available between the hours of 8:30 a.m. and 6 p.m., Eastern Time, to discuss premium payments, insurance dividends, address changes, policy loans, naming beneficiaries and reporting the death of the insured.

If the insurance policy number is not known, send whatever information is available, such as the veteran's VA file number, date of birth, Social Security number, military serial number or military service branch and dates of service to:

> Department of Veterans Affairs
> Regional Office and Insurance Center
> Box 42954
> Philadelphia, PA 19101

## Servicemembers' Group Life Insurance (SGLI)

The following are automatically insured for $400,000 under Servicemembers' Group Life Insurance (SGLI):

1. Active-duty members of the Army, Navy, Air Force, Marines

> and Coast Guard.
> 2. Commissioned members of the National Oceanic and Atmospheric Administration and the Public Health Service.
> 3. Cadets or midshipmen of the service academies.
> 4. Members, cadets and midshipmen of the ROTC while engaged in authorized training.
> 5. Members of the Ready Reserves.
> 6. Members who volunteer for assignment to a mobilization category in the Individual Ready Reserve or Inactive National Guard.

Individuals may elect in writing to be covered for a lesser amount or not at all. Part-time coverage may be provided to reservists who do not qualify for full-time coverage. Premiums are automatically deducted from the servicemember's pay. At the time of separation from service, SGLI can be converted to either Veterans' Group Life Insurance (VGLI) or a commercial plan through participating companies. SGLI coverage continues for 120 days after separation at no charge.

Coverage of $10,000 is also automatically provided for dependent children of members insured under SGLI with no premium required.

# Traumatic Servicemembers' Group Life Insurance (TSGLI)

Members of the armed services serve our nation heroically during times of great need, but what happens when they experience great needs of their own because they have sustained a traumatic injury? Traumatic Servicemembers' Group Life Insurance (TSGLI) helps severely injured servicemembers through their time of need with a one-time payment.  The amount varies depending on the injury, but it could be the difference that allows their families to be with them during their recovery; helps them with unforeseen expenses; or gives them a financial head start on life after recovery.

TSGLI is an insurance program that is bundled with Servicemembers' Group Life Insurance (SGLI) and an additional $1.00 has been added to the servicemember's SGLI premium to cover TSGLI.  After Dec. 1, 2005, all servicemembers who are covered by SGLI are eligible for TSGLI coverage, regardless of where their qualifying traumatic injury occurred.  However, TSGLI claims require approval.  In addition, there is a retroactive program that covers servicemembers who sustained a qualifying traumatic injury while in theater supporting Operation Enduring Freedom (OEF),  Operation Iraqi Freedom (OIF), or while on orders in a Combat Zone Tax Exclusion (CZTE) area from Oct. 7, 2001, through Nov. 30, 2005.

For more information, visit the website at http://www.insurance. va.gov/sgliSite/TSGLI/TSGLI.htm, or call 1-800-237-1336 (Army); 1-800-368-3202 (Navy); 1-703-432-9277 (Marine Corps); 1-210-565-3310 or 2410 (Air Force); and 1-202-267-1648 (Coast Guard).

# Family Servicemembers' Group Life Insurance (FSGLI)

Family Servicemembers' Group Life Insurance (FSGLI) provides up to $100,000 of life insurance coverage for spouses, not to exceed the amount of SGLI the insured member has in force. FSGLI is a servicemembers' benefit, and the member pays the premium and is the beneficiary of the policy. If a servicemember drops his or her SGLI coverage, leaves the military, or divorces the spouse, the spouse's policy can be converted to a private life insurance policy within 120 days of the date SGLI coverage ended or the date of divorce.

# Veterans' Group Life Insurance (VGLI)

SGLI may be converted to Veterans' Group Life Insurance (VGLI), which provides renewable term coverage to:

1. Veterans with full-time SGLI coverage upon release from active duty or the reserves.
2. Veterans with part-time SGLI coverage who incur a disability or aggravate a pre-existing disability during a reserve period that renders them uninsurable at standard premium rates.
3. Members of the Individual Ready Reserve and Inactive National Guard.

SGLI can be converted to VGLI up to the amount of coverage the servicemember had when separated from service. Veterans who submit an application and the initial premium within 120 days of leaving the service will be covered regardless of their health. After 120 days, veterans can still convert to VGLI if they submit an application, pay the initial premium, and show evidence of insurability within one year of termination of SGLI coverage.

Servicemembers who are totally disabled at the time of separation are eligible for free SGLI Disability Extension of up to two years. Those covered under the SGLI Disability Extension are automatically converted to VGLI at the end of their extension period. VGLI is convertible at any time to a permanent plan policy with any participating commercial insurance company.

## Accelerated Death Benefits Available to Terminally Ill Policyholders

SGLI, FSGLI and VGLI policyholders who are terminally ill (prognosis of nine months or less to live) can receive up to 50 percent of their coverage amount in advance.   This option may be requested one time only.

## Service-Disabled Veterans' Insurance (S-DVI)

A veteran who was discharged under other than dishonorable conditions and who has a service-connected disability but is otherwise in good health may apply to VA for up to $10,000 in life insurance coverage under the Service-Disabled Veterans' Insurance (S-DVI) program. Applications must be submitted within two years from the date of being notified of the approval of a new service-connected disability by VA.  This insurance is limited to veterans who left service on or after April 25, 1951.

Veterans who are totally disabled may apply for a waiver of premiums and additional supplemental coverage of up to $20,000. However, premiums cannot be waived on the additional insurance. To be eligible for this type of supplemental insurance, veterans must meet all of the following four requirements:

1. Be under age 65.
2. Meet the requirements for total disability.
3. Have an S-DVI policy with premiums waived due to total disability.
4. Apply for additional insurance within one year from the date of notification of waiver approval on the S-DVI policy.

# Veterans' Mortgage Life Insurance (VMLI)

Veterans' Mortgage Life Insurance (VMLI) is available to severely disabled veterans who have been approved for a Specially Adapted Housing Grant. Maximum coverage is $90,000, and is only payable to the mortgage company. Protection is issued automatically, provided the veteran submits information required to establish a premium and does not decline coverage. Coverage automatically terminates when the mortgage is paid off.

If a mortgage is disposed of through sale of the property, VMLI may be obtained on the mortgage of another home.

# Insurance Dividends Issued Annually

World War I, World War II, and Korean-era veterans with active policies beginning with the letters V, RS, W, J, JR, JS, or K are issued tax-free dividends annually on the policy anniversary date. Policyholders do not need to apply for dividends, but may select from among the following dividend options:

1. **Cash:**  The dividend is paid directly to the insured either by a mailed check or by direct deposit.
2. **Paid-Up Additional Insurance:**  The dividend is used to purchase additional insurance coverage.
3. **Credit or Deposit:**  The dividend is held in an account for the policyholder with interest. Withdrawals from the account can be made at any time.  The interest rate may be adjusted each year.
4. **Net Premium Billing Options:** These options use the dividend to pay the annual policy premium. If the dividend exceeds the premium, the policyholder has options to choose how the remainder is used.  If the dividend is not enough to pay an annual premium, the policyholder is billed for the balance.
5. **Dividend Options:**  Dividends can also be used to repay a loan or pay premiums in advance, be left on-account as a deposit earning interest, or paid to a bank account.

# Other Insurance Information

The following information applies to policies issued to World War II, Korean, and Vietnam-era veterans and any Service-Disabled Veterans Insurance policies.  Policies in this group are prefixed by the letters K, V, RS, W-J, JR, JS, or RH.

**Reinstating Lapsed Insurance:** Lapsed term policies may be reinstated within five years from the date of lapse. A five-year term policy that is not lapsed at the end of the term is automatically renewed for an additional five years. Lapsed permanent plans may be reinstated within certain time limits and with certain health requirements. Reinstated permanent plan policies require repayment of all back premiums, plus interest.

**Converting Term Policies:** Term policies are renewed automatically every five years, with premiums increasing at each renewal. Premiums do not increase after age 70.  Term policies may be converted to permanent plans, which have fixed premiums for life and earn cash and loan values.

**Paid-up Insurance Available on Term Policies:** Effective September 2000, VA provides paid-up insurance on term policies whose premiums have been capped. Veterans who have National Service Life Insurance (NSLI) term insurance (renewal age 71 or older) and stop paying premiums on their policies will be given a termination dividend. This dividend will be used to purchase a reduced amount of paid-up insurance, which insures the veteran for life and no premium payments are required. The amount of insurance remains level.  This does not apply to S-DVI (RH) policies.

**Disability Provisions:** National Service Life Insurance (NSLI) policyholders who become totally disabled before age 65 should ask VA about premium waivers.

**Borrowing on Policies:** Policyholders with permanent plan policies may borrow up to 94 percent of the cash surrender value of their insurance. Interest is compounded annually. The loan interest rate is variable and may be obtained by calling toll-free 1-800-669-8477.

# *Chapter 7*

# Burial and Memorial Benefits

*Eligibility, Burial in VA National Cemeteries, Inscribed Headstones and Markers, Burial Flags Furnished by VA, Reimbursement of Burial Expenses, Military Funeral Honors Provided by DOD Upon Request, Veterans Cemeteries Administered by Other Agencies*

## Eligibility

Veterans discharged from active duty under conditions other than dishonorable and servicemembers who die while on active duty, as well as spouses and dependent children of veterans and active duty servicemembers, may be eligible for VA burial and memorial benefits. The veteran does not have to pre-decease a spouse or dependent child for them to be eligible.

With certain exceptions, active duty service beginning after Sept. 7, 1980, as an enlisted person, and after Oct. 16, 1981, as an officer, must be for a minimum of 24 consecutive months or the full period of active duty (as in the case of reservists or National Guard members called to active duty for a limited duration). Eligibility is not established by active duty for training in the reserves or National Guard.

Reservists and National Guard members, as well as their spouses and dependent children, are eligible if they were entitled to retired pay at the time of death, or would have been if they were over age 60.

VA national cemetery directors verify eligibility for burial in their cemeteries. A copy of the veteran's discharge document that specifies the period(s) of active duty and character of discharge, along with the deceased's death certificate and proof of relationship to the veteran (for eligible family members) are all that are usually needed to determine eligibility.

This chapter contains information on the full range of VA burial and memorial benefits. Readers with questions should contact the nearest national cemetery, listed by state in the VA Facilities section of this book, call 1-800-827-1000, or visit the website at http://www.cem.va.gov/.

## Burial in VA National Cemeteries

Burial in a VA national cemetery is available for eligible veterans, their spouses and dependents at no cost to the family and includes the gravesite, grave-liner, opening and closing of the grave, a headstone or marker, and perpetual care as part of a national shrine. For veterans, benefits also include a burial flag (with case for active duty) and military funeral honors. Family members and other loved ones of deceased veterans may request Presidential Memorial Certificates.

VA operates 124 national cemeteries, of which 84 are open for new interments and 20 of these accept only cremated remains. Burial options are limited to those available at a specific cemetery but may include in-ground casket, or interment of cremated remains in a columbarium, in ground or in a scatter garden. Contact the nearest national cemetery to determine if it is open for new burials and which options are available.

Seven new national cemeteries are scheduled to open in the next few years near the cities of Bakersfield, Calif.; Birmingham, Ala.; Greenville, S.C.; Jacksonville, Fla.; Philadelphia, Pa.; Sarasota, Fla.; and West Palm Beach, Fla.

The funeral director or the next of kin makes interment arrangements by contacting the national cemetery in which burial is desired. VA normally does not conduct burials on weekends. Gravesites cannot be reserved; however VA will honor reservations made under previous programs.

Surviving spouses of veterans who died on or after Jan.1, 2000, do not lose eligibility for burial in a national cemetery if they remarry. Burial of dependent children is limited to unmarried children under 21 years of age, or under 23 years of age if a full-time student at an approved educational institution. Unmarried adult children who become physically or mentally disabled and incapable of self-support before age 21, or age 23 if a full-time student, also are eligible for burial.

# VA Provides Inscribed Headstones and Markers for Veterans' Graves

Veterans, active duty servicemembers, retired reservists, and National Guard servicemembers are eligible for an inscribed headstone or marker to mark their grave at any cemetery -- national, state veterans, or private.  The headstone or marker will be delivered at no cost, anywhere in the world. Spouses and dependent children are eligible for a government headstone or marker only if they are buried in a national or state veterans cemetery.

Flat markers are available in bronze, granite or marble. Upright headstones come in granite or marble. In national cemeteries, the style chosen must be consistent with existing monuments at the place of burial. Niche markers are available to mark columbaria used for inurnment of cremated remains.

Headstones and markers previously provided by the government may be replaced at the government's expense if badly deteriorated, illegible, vandalized or stolen. To check the status of an application for a headstone or marker for a national or state veterans cemetery, call the cemetery. To check the status of one being placed in a private cemetery, call 1-800-697-6947.

**Inscription:** Headstones and markers must be inscribed with the name of the deceased, branch of service, and year of birth and death. They also may be inscribed with other markings, including an authorized emblem of belief and, space permitting, additional text including military rank; war service such as "World War II;" complete dates of birth and death; military awards; military organizations; civilian or veteran affiliations; and words of endearment.

**Private Cemeteries:** To apply for a headstone or marker for a private cemetery, mail a completed VA Form 40-1330 (available at http://www.va.gov/vaforms/va/pdf/VA40-1330.pdf), Application for Standard Government Headstone or Marker for Installation in a Private Cemetery or a State Veterans' Cemetery, and a copy of the veteran's military discharge document and death certificate to Memorial Programs Service (41A1), Department of Veterans Affairs, 5109 Russell Rd., Quantico, VA  22134-3903. Or fax documents to 1-800-455-7143.

For veteran deaths occurring on or after Sept. 11, 2001, VA will provide a government headstone or marker even if the grave is already marked with a private one. Before ordering, check with the cemetery to ensure that the additional headstone or marker will be accepted. Any placement fee will not be reimbursed by VA.

**"In Memory Of" Markers:** VA provides memorial headstones and markers, bearing the inscription "In Memory Of" as the first line, to memorialize those whose remains were not recovered or identified, were buried at sea, donated to science or cremated and scattered. Eligibility is the same for regular headstones and markers. There is no fee when the "In Memory Of" marker is placed in a national cemetery. Any fees associated with placement in another cemetery will not be reimbursed by VA.

# Presidential Memorial Certificates Issued to Next of Kin Upon Request

Certificates are issued upon request to recognize the military service of honorably discharged deceased veterans. Next of kin, relatives and friends may request them in person at any VA regional office or by mail: Presidential Memorial Certificates (41A1C), Department of Veterans Affairs, 5109 Russell Rd., Quantico, VA 22143-3903. Or fax documents to 202-565-8054.

No form is required and there is no time limit for requesting a certificate(s), but requests should include a copy of the veteran's discharge document and death certificate and clearly indicate to what address the certificate(s) should be sent. Information and a sample certificate can be found at http://www.cem.va.gov/cem/pmc.asp.

# Burial Flags Furnished by VA

VA will furnish a U.S. burial flag for memorialization of:

1. Veterans who served during wartime or after Jan. 31, 1955.
2. Veterans who were entitled to retired pay for service in the reserves, or would have been entitled if over age 60.
3. Members or former members of the Selected Reserve who served their initial obligation, or were discharged for a disability incurred or aggravated in line of duty, or died while a member of the Selected Reserve.

# Reimbursement of Burial Expenses

VA will pay a burial allowance up to $2,000 if the veteran's death is service-connected. In such cases, the person who bore the veteran's burial expenses may claim reimbursement from VA.

In some cases, VA will pay the cost of transporting the remains of a service-connected veteran to the nearest national cemetery with available gravesites. There is no time limit for filing reimbursement claims in service-connected death cases.

**Burial Allowance:** VA will pay a $300 burial and funeral allowance for veterans who, at time of death, were entitled to receive pension or compensation or would have been entitled if they weren't receiving military retirement pay. Eligibility also may be established when death occurs in a VA facility, a VA-contracted nursing home or a state veterans nursing home. In non service-connected death cases, claims must be filed within two years after burial or cremation.

**Plot Allowance:** VA will pay a $300 plot allowance when a veteran is buried in a cemetery not under U.S. government jurisdiction if: the veteran was discharged from active duty because of disability incurred or aggravated in the line of duty; the veteran was receiving compensation or pension or would have been if they weren't receiving military retired pay; or they died in a VA facility.

The $300 plot allowance may be paid to the state for the cost of a plot or interment in a state-owned cemetery reserved solely for veteran burials if the veteran is buried without charge. Burial ex-

penses paid by the deceased's employer or a state agency will not
be reimbursed.

# Military Funeral Honors Provided by DOD Upon Request at Veterans' Funerals

Upon request, DOD will provide military funeral honors consisting
of folding and presentation of the United States flag and the playing
of "Taps." A funeral honors detail consists of two or more uniformed
members of the armed forces, with at least one member from the
deceased's branch of service.

Family members should inform their funeral directors if they want military funeral honors. DOD maintains a toll-free number (1-877-MIL-
HONR) for use by funeral directors only to request honors. VA can
help arrange honors for burials at VA national cemeteries. Veterans'
service organizations or volunteer groups may help provide honors.
For more information, visit http://www.militaryfuneralhonors.osd.mil/.

# Veterans Cemeteries Administered by Other Agencies

**Arlington National Cemetery:** Administered by the Department of
the Army. Eligibility is more restrictive than at VA national cemeteries.
For information, call (703) 607-8000, write Superintendent, Arlington
National Cemetery, Arlington, VA 22211, or visit http://www.arlington-
cemetery.org/.

**State Veterans Cemeteries:** Sixty-three state veterans cemeteries
offer burial options for veterans and their families. These cemeteries
have similar eligibility requirements but usually require some residence. Some services, particularly for family members, may require
a fee. Contact the state cemetery or state veterans affairs office for
information. To locate a state veterans cemetery, visit http://www.
cem.va.gov/cem/scg/lsvc.asp.

**Department of the Interior:** Administers two active national cemeteries: Andersonville National Cemetery in Georgia and Andrew
Johnson National Cemetery in Tennessee. Eligibility is similar to VA
cemeteries.

# *Chapter 8*

# Reserve and National Guard

*Eligibility for VA Benefits, Qualifying for VA Health Care, Disability Benefits, Educational Benefits Under Montgomery GI Bill – Selected Reserve, Reserve Educational Assistance Program, Re-employment Rights of Veterans Under the Law*

## Eligibility for VA Benefits

Reservists who served on active duty establish veteran status and may be eligible for the full-range of VA benefits, depending on the length of active military service and a discharge or release from active duty under conditions other than dishonorable. In addition, reservists not activated may qualify for some VA benefits.

National Guard members can establish eligibility for VA benefits if activated for federal service during a period of war or domestic emergency. Activation for other than federal service does not qualify guard members for all VA benefits. Claims for VA benefits based on federal service filed by members of the National Guard should include a copy of the military orders, presidential proclamation or executive order that clearly demonstrates the federal nature of the service.

# Qualifying for VA Health Care

Reservists and National Guard members activated for federal service can qualify for VA health care, but generally must be enrolled to receive services. See Chapter 1, "VA Health Care," for details on enrollment and services.

Reservists and National Guard members who served on active duty in a theater of combat operations during a period of war after the Gulf War, or in combat against a hostile force after Nov. 11, 1998, are eligible for enrollment in Priority Group 6 unless otherwise eligible for enrollment in a higher priority group and free health care services for conditions potentially related to combat service for two years following separation from active duty. For information, call 1-877-222-VETS (8387).

# Qualifying for VA Disability Benefits

VA pays monthly compensation benefits for service-connected disabilities – those incurred or aggravated during active duty and active duty for training, and for residuals of heart attack or stroke that occurred during inactive duty for training. For additional information see Chapter 2, "Veterans with Service-Connected Disabilities".

# Educational Benefits Under the Montgomery GI Bill – Selected Reserve

Members of reserve elements of the Army, Navy, Air Force, Marine Corps and Coast Guard, and members of the Army National Guard and the Air National Guard, may be entitled to up to 36 months of educational benefits under the Montgomery GI Bill (MGIB) – Selected Reserve. To be eligible, the participant must:

1. Have a six-year obligation in the Selected Reserve or National Guard signed after June 30, 1985, or, if an officer, agree to serve six years in addition to the original obligation.
2. Complete initial active duty for training.
3. Have a high school diploma or equivalency certificate before applying for benefits.

4.  Remain in good standing in a Selected Reserve or National
    Guard unit.

Reserve components determine eligibility for benefits. VA does not
make decisions about eligibility and cannot make payments until the
reserve component has determined eligibility and notified VA.

**Period of Eligibility:** Benefits generally end the day a reservist or
National Guard member separates from military service. However,
if you leave the Selected Reserve, you may still be eligible for a full
10 years from the date you became eligible (if you became eligible
before Oct. 1, 1992), or a full 14 years from the date you became
eligible on or after Oct. 1, 1992.  You may be eligible if you were
separated because you had a disability that was not caused by misconduct,  your unit was inactivated, or you were otherwise involun-
tarily separated during the period from Oct. 1, 1991, through Dec. 31,
2001.

If you stayed in the Selected Reserve, VA can generally extend your
eligibility period if you were called up to active duty.  In this case, VA
will extend your eligibility by the period of your active duty service
plus four months.

**Payments:** The rate for full-time training effective Oct. 1, 2006, is
$309 a month for 36 months. Part-time benefits are reduced propor-
tionately. For complete current rates, visit http://www.gibill.va.gov/.
DOD may make additional contributions.

**Training:** Participants may take undergraduate or technical training
at colleges and universities. Those who have a six-year commitment
beginning after Sept. 30, 1990, may also take the following training:
graduate courses; State licensure and certification; courses for a
certificate or diploma from business, technical or vocational schools;
cooperative training; apprenticeship or on-the-job training; correspondence courses; independent study programs; flight training; entrepreneurship training; or remedial, deficiency or refresher courses
needed to complete a program of study.

**Work-Study:** Participants may be eligible for a work-study program
in which they work for VA and receive hourly wages. Veterans must
train at the three-quarter or full-time rate. The work allowed includes:

1. Outreach services for VA.
2. VA paperwork.
3. Work at national or state veterans' cemeteries.
4. Work at VA medical centers or state veterans homes.
5. Other VA approved activities.

**Counseling:** VA counseling is available to help determine educational or vocational strengths and weaknesses and plan education or employment goals.  Additionally, those ineligible for MGIB may still receive VA counseling beginning 180 days prior to separation from active duty through the first full year following honorable discharge.

# Reserve Educational Assistance Program

This program provides educational assistance to members of National Guard and reserve components – Selected Reserve and Individual Ready Reserve (IRR) – who are called or ordered to active duty service in response to a war or national emergency as declared by the president or Congress.  Visit www.gibill.va.gov/ for more information.

**Eligibility:** Eligibility is determined by DOD or the Department of Homeland Security. Generally, a servicemember who serves on active duty on or after Sept. 11, 2001, for at least 90 consecutive days is eligible.

**Payments:** The educational payment rate is based on the number of continuous days of active duty service performed by the Reservist or National Guard servicemember.  Full-time students receive payments on a monthly basis.

| 2007 Reserve Educational Assistance Program Educational Payment Rates* | |
| --- | --- |
| **Length of Active-Duty Service for Reservists and National Guard Servicemembers** | **Monthly Payment Rate for Full-Time Students** |
| 90 days but less than one year | $430.00 |
| One year but less then two years | $645.00 |
| Two or more continuous years | $860.00 |

*As of Oct. 1, 2006*

**Training:** Approved training includes graduate and undergraduate degrees, vocational/technical training, on-the-job or apprenticeship training, correspondence training, and flight training. Licensing and certification test reimbursement is effective Jan. 6, 2006.

**Period of Eligibility:** Members of the Selected Reserve called to active duty are eligible as long as they continue to serve in the Selected Reserve. They lose eligibility if they go into the IRR. Members of the IRR called to active duty are eligible as long as they stay in the IRR or the Selected Reserve.

Members who are separated from the IRR or the Selected Reserve for a disability, which was not the result of willful misconduct, are entitled to benefits for 10 years after the date of eligibility.

## Eligibility for VA Home Loan Guaranty

National Guard members and reservists are eligible for a VA home loan if they have completed at least six years of honorable service, are mobilized for active duty service for a period of at least 90 days, or were discharged because of a service-connected disability.

Reservists who do not qualify for VA housing loan benefits may be eligible for loans on favorable terms insured by the Federal Housing Administration (FHA), part of HUD.  Additional information can be found in Chapter 5 -- "Home Loan Guaranty" – of this publication.

## Eligibility for Life Insurance

National Guard members and reservists are eligible to receive Servicemembers' Group Life Insurance, Veterans' Group Life Insurance, and Family Servicemembers' Group Life Insurance. They may also be eligible for Traumatic Servicemembers' Group Life Insurance or Service-Disabled Veterans Insurance if called to active duty and injured with a service-connected disability, and Veterans' Mortgage Life Insurance if approved for a Specially Adapted Housing Grant. Complete details can be found in Chapter 6 -- "VA Life Insurance" – of this publication.

## VA Provides Burial and Memorial Benefits

VA provides a burial flag for memorialization of members or former members of the Selected Reserve who served their initial obligation, or were discharged for a disability incurred or aggravated in line of duty, or died while a member of the Selected Reserve. Information on benefits and eligibility can be found in Chapter 7 -- "Burial and Memorial Benefits" – of this publication.

## Re-employment Rights of Veterans Returning to Civilian Jobs Under the Law

A person who left a civilian job to enter active duty in the armed forces is entitled to return to the job after discharge or release from active duty if they:

1.  Gave advance notice of military service to the employer.
2.  Did not exceed five years cumulative absence from the civilian job (with some exceptions).
3.  Submitted a timely application for re-employment.
4.  Did not receive a dishonorable or other punitive discharge.

The law calls for a returning veteran to be placed in the job as if they had never left, including benefits based on seniority such as pensions, pay increases and promotions. The law also prohibits discrimination in hiring, promotion or other advantages of employment on the basis of military service.

Veterans seeking re-employment should apply, verbally or in writing, to the company's hiring official and keep a record of their application. If problems arise, contact the Department of Labor's Veterans' Employment and Training Service (VETS) in the state of the employer.

Federal employees not properly re-employed may appeal directly to the Merit Systems Protection Board. Non-federal employees may file complaints in U.S. District Court. For information, visit http://www.dol.gov/vets/programs/userra/main.htm.

# Chapter 9

# Special Groups of Veterans

*Women Veterans, VA Conducts Outreach and Provides Programs
to Homeless Veterans, World War II Era Filipino Veterans Eligible
for Certain VA Benefits, VA Benefits Available to Veterans Living or
Traveling Overseas,  Impact of Incarceration on VA Benefits*

## Women Veterans

Women veterans are eligible for the same VA benefits as male veterans, but can also receive additional gender-specific services, including breast and pelvic examinations and other reproductive health care services.

VA provides preventive health care counseling, contraceptive services, menopause management, Pap smears and mammography. Referrals are made for services that VA is unable to provide. Women Veterans' Program Managers are available in a private setting at all VA facilities to help women veterans seeking treatment and benefits. For information, visit http://www.va.gov/womenvet/.

VA health care professionals provide counseling and treatment to help veterans overcome psychological issues resulting from sexual trauma that occurred while serving on active duty, or active duty for training if service was in the National Guard or reserves. Veterans who are not otherwise eligible for VA health care may still receive these services and do not need to enroll. Appropriate services are provided for any injury, illness or psychological condition resulting from such trauma.

# VA Conducts Outreach and Provides Programs to Help Homeless Veterans

VA provides comprehensive medical, psychological and rehabilitation treatment for eligible homeless veterans and conducts homeless outreach such as community-based "stand downs" to help homeless veterans. Many VA benefits, including disability compensation, pension and education can help at-risk veterans avoid homelessness.

Other programs for homeless veterans include residential rehabilitation services at VA domiciliaries, therapeutic group homes, special day centers, and comprehensive homeless centers. For assistance, contact the nearest VA medical facility or visit http://www.va.gov/homeless/ to find contact information on VA homeless veteran coordinators in each state.

VA also provides grant and per diem funds to community agencies providing services to homeless veterans. The grant program pays up to 65 percent of the cost of construction, renovation, or acquisition of a building for use as service centers or transitional housing for homeless veterans, or for the purchase of vans for the transportation of homeless veterans. The per diem provides funding for operational costs. Call toll-free 1-877-332-0334 or visit http://www.va.gov/homeless/.

The Department of Labor provides employment and training services, as well as grants to community organizations that provide counseling, job search and placement assistance, remedial education and on-the-job training for homeless veterans. For information, call 202-693-4700 or visit http://www.dol.gov/vets/welcome.html.

# World War II Era Filipino Veterans Are Eligible for Certain VA Benefits

World War II era Filipino veterans are eligible for certain VA benefits. Generally, Old Philippine Scouts are eligible for VA benefits in the same manner as U.S. veterans. Commonwealth Army veterans, including certain organized Filipino guerrilla forces and New Philippine Scouts residing in the United States who are citizens or lawfully admitted for permanent residence, are also eligible for VA health care in the United States on the same basis as U.S. veterans.

Certain Commonwealth Army veterans and new Philippine Scouts may be eligible for disability compensation and burial benefits. Other veterans of recognized guerrilla groups also may be eligible for certain VA benefits. Survivors of World War II era Filipino veterans may be eligible for dependency and indemnity compensation. Eligibility and the rates of benefits vary based on the recipient's citizenship and place of residence. Call 1-800-827-1000 for additional information.

## VA Benefits Are Available to Veterans Living or Traveling Overseas

VA will pay for medical services to treat service-connected disabilities and related conditions or for medical services needed as part of a vocational rehabilitation program for veterans living or traveling outside the United States. Veterans living in the Philippines should register with the U.S. Veterans Affairs office in Pasay City, telephone 011-632-833-4566. All other veterans living or planning to travel outside the U.S. should register with the Denver Foreign Medical Program office, P.O. Box 65021, Denver, CO 80206-9021, USA; telephone 303-331-7590.   More information about the Foreign Medical Program is available on the program Web site at http://www.va.gov/hac/forbeneficiaries/fmp/fmp.asp.

Some veterans traveling or living overseas can telephone the Foreign Medical Program toll free from these countries:  Germany 0800-1800-011; Australia 1800-354-965; Italy 800-782-655; United Kingdom (England and Scotland) 0800-032-7425; Mexico 001-877-345-8179; Japan 00531-13-0871; Costa Rica 0800-013-0759; and Spain 900-981-776.  (Note:  Veterans in Mexico or Costa Rica must first dial the United States country code.)

VA monetary benefits, including disability compensation, pension, educational benefits, and burial allowances, generally are payable overseas. Some programs are restricted. Home loan guaranties are available only in the United States and selected U.S. territories and possessions. Educational benefits are limited to approved, degree-granting programs in institutions of higher learning.

Beneficiaries living in foreign countries should contact the nearest

American embassy or consulate for help. In Canada, contact an office of Veterans Affairs Canada. For information visit http://www.vba.va.gov/bln/21/foreign/index.htm.

## World War II Era Merchant Marine Seamen May Qualify for VA Benefits

Certain Merchant Marine seamen who served in World War II may qualify for veterans' benefits. When applying for medical care, seamen must present their discharge certificate from the Department of Defense. Call 1-800-827-1000 for help obtaining a certificate.

## VA May Provide Medical Care to Certain Allied Veterans Who Served During WWI or WWII

VA may provide medical care to certain veterans of nations allied or associated with the United States during World War I or World War II if authorized and reimbursed by the foreign government. VA also may provide hospitalization, outpatient care, and domiciliary care to former members of the armed forces of Czechoslovakia or Poland who fought in World War I or World War II in armed conflict against an enemy of the United States if they have been U.S. citizens for at least 10 years.

## World War Service by Particular Groups Qualifies Them for VA Benefits

A number of groups who provided military-related service to the United States can receive VA benefits. A discharge by the Secretary of Defense is needed to qualify. Service in the following groups has been certified as active military service for benefits purposes:

1. Women Air Force Service Pilots (WASPs).

2. World War I Signal Corps Female Telephone Operators Unit.

3. World War I Engineer Field Clerks.

4. Women's Army Auxiliary Corps (WAAC).

5. Quartermaster Corps female clerical employees serving with the American Expeditionary Forces in World War I.

6. Civilian employees of Pacific naval air bases who actively participated in defense of Wake Island during World War II.

7. Reconstruction aides and dietitians in World War I.

8. Male civilian ferry pilots.

9. Wake Island defenders from Guam.

10. Civilian personnel assigned to OSS secret intelligence.

11. Guam Combat Patrol.

12. Quartermaster Corps members of the Keswick crew on Corregidor during World War II.

13. U.S. civilians who participated in the defense of Bataan.

14. U.S. merchant seamen who served on block ships in support of Operation Mulberry in the World War II invasion of Normandy.

15. American merchant marines in oceangoing service during World War II.

16. Civilian Navy IFF radar technicians who served in combat areas of the Pacific during World War II.

17. U.S. civilians of the American Field Service who served overseas in World War I.

18. U.S. civilians of the American Field Service who served overseas under U.S. armies and U.S. army groups in World War II.

19. U.S. civilian employees of American Airlines who served overseas in a contract with the Air Transport Command between Dec. 14, 1941, and Aug. 14, 1945.

20. Civilian crewmen of U.S. Coast and Geodetic Survey
    vessels  who served in areas of immediate military
    hazard while conducting cooperative operations with and
    for the U.S. armed forces between Dec. 7, 1941, and Aug.
    15, 1945.  Qualifying vessels are: the Derickson,
    Explorer, Gilber, Hilgard, E. Lester Jones, Lydonia Patton,
    Surveyor, Wainwright, Westdahl, Oceanographer,
    Hydrographer and Pathfinder.

21. Members of the American Volunteer Group (Flying Tigers)
    who served between Dec. 7, 1941, and July 18, 1942.

22. U.S. civilian flight crew and aviation ground support
    employees of United Air Lines who served overseas in a
    contract with Air Transport Command between Dec. 14,
    1941, and Aug. 14, 1945.

23. U.S. civilian flight crew, including pursers, and aviation ground
    support employees of Transcontinental and Western Air, Inc.
    (TWA), who served overseas in a contract with the Air Trans-
    port Command between Dec. 14, 1941, and Aug. 14, 1945.

24. U.S. civilian flight crew and aviation ground support
    employees of Consolidated Vultee Aircraft Corp. who
    served overseas in a contract with Air Transport Command
    between Dec. 14, 1941, and Aug. 14, 1945.

25. U.S. civilian flight crew and aviation ground support employees
    of Pan American World Airways and its subsidiaries and affili-
    ates, who served overseas in a contract with the Air Transport
    Command and Naval Air Transport Service between Dec. 14,
    1941, and Aug. 14, 1945.

26. Honorably discharged members of the American Volunteer
    Guard, Eritrea Service Command, between June 21, 1942,
    and March 31, 1943.

27. U.S. civilian flight crew and aviation ground support
    employees of Northwest Airlines who served overseas under
    the airline's contract with Air Transport Command from
    Dec. 14, 1941, through Aug. 14, 1945.

28. U.S. civilian female employees of the U.S. Army Nurse Corps who served in the defense of Bataan and Corregidor during the period Jan. 2, 1942, to Feb. 3, 1945.

29. U.S. flight crew and aviation ground support employees of Northeast Airlines Atlantic Division, who served overseas as a result of Northeast Airlines' contract with the Air Transport Command during the period Dec. 7, 1941, through Aug. 14, 1945.

30. U.S. civilian flight crew and aviation ground support employees of Braniff Airways, who served overseas in the North Atlantic or under the jurisdiction of the North Atlantic Wing, Air Transport Command, as a result of a contract with the Air Transport Command during the period Feb. 26, 1942, through Aug. 14, 1945.

31. Chamorro and Carolina former native police who received military training in the Donnal area of central Saipan and were placed under command of Lt. Casino of the 6th Provisional Military Police Battalion to accompany U.S. Marines on active, combat patrol from Aug. 19, 1945, to Sept. 2, 1945.

32. The operational Analysis Group of the Office of Scientific Research and Development, Office of Emergency Management, which served overseas with the U.S. Army Air Corps from Dec. 7, 1941, through Aug. 15, 1945.

33. Service as a member of the Alaska Territorial Guard during World War II of any individual who was honorably discharged under section 8147 of the Department of Defense Appropriations Act of 2001.

# Impact of Incarceration, Outstanding Felony Warrants on Beneficiary's VA Benefits

VA benefits are affected if a beneficiary is convicted of a felony and imprisoned for more than 60 days.

Disability or Death Pension paid to an incarcerated beneficiary must be discontinued. Disability compensation paid to an incarcerated veteran rated 20 percent or more disabled is limited to the 10 percent rate. For a surviving spouse, child or dependent parent receiving Dependency and Indemnity Compensation, or a veteran whose disability rating is 10 percent, the payment is reduced to half of the rate payable to a veteran evaluated as 10 percent disabled.

Any amounts not paid may be apportioned to eligible dependents. Payments are not reduced for participants in work-release programs, residing in halfway houses or under community control.

Failure to notify VA of a veteran's incarceration can result in overpayment of benefits and the subsequent loss of all VA financial benefits until the overpayment is recovered. VA benefits will not be provided to any veteran or dependent wanted for an outstanding felony warrant. Persons convicted of a federal or state capital crime are barred from receiving VA burial benefits.

# *Chapter 10*

# Transition Assistance

*VA Seamless Transition, Transition Assistance Program, Veterans' Workforce Investment, State Employment Services, Veterans Receive Preference When Applying for Federal Jobs, Center for Veterans Enterprise Helps Veterans Form Small Businesses*

## VA Seamless Transition

VA has stationed personnel at major military hospitals to help seriously injured servicemembers returning from OEF and OIF as they transition from military to civilian life. OEF/OIF servicemembers who have questions about VA benefits or need assistance in filing a VA claim or accessing services can contact the nearest VA office or call 1-800-827-1000.

## Transition Assistance Program

The Transition Assistance Program (TAP) consists of comprehensive three-day workshops at military installations designed to help servicemembers as they transition from military to civilian life. The program includes job search, employment and training information, as well as VA benefits information, to servicemembers who are within 12 months of separation or 24 months of retirement.

A companion workshop, the Disabled Transition Assistance Program, provides information on VA's Vocational Rehabilitation and Employment Program, as well as other programs for the disabled.

Additional information about these programs is available at http://www.dol.gov/vets/programs/tap/tap_fs.htm.

# Miliary Services Provide Pre-Separation Counseling to Servicemembers

Servicemembers may receive pre-separation counseling 24 months prior to retirement or 12 months prior to separation from active duty. These sessions present information on education, training, employment assistance, National Guard and reserve programs, medical benefits and financial assistance.

# Obtaining Verification of Military Experience and Training Document

The Verification of Military Experience and Training (VMET) Document, DD Form 2586, helps servicemembers verify previous experience and training to potential employers, negotiate credits at schools and obtain certificates or licenses. VMET documents are available only through Army, Navy, Air Force and Marine Corps Transition Support offices and are intended for service members who have at least six months of active service. Servicemembers should obtain VMET documents from their Transition Support office within 12 months of separation or 24 months of retirement.

# Veterans Can Find Calendar Items, Business Opportunities on Transition Bulletin Board

To find business opportunities, a calendar of transition seminars, job fairs, information on veterans associations, transition services, training and education opportunities, as well as other announcements, visit the website at http://www.dmdc.osd.mil/ot/.

# DOD Transportal Offers Veterans Links to Job Search and Recruiting Web Sites

To find locations and phone numbers of all Transition Assistance Offices as well as mini-courses on conducting successful job search campaigns, writing resumes, using the Internet to find a job, and links to job search and recruiting Web sites, visit the DOD Transportal at http://www.dodtransportal.org/.

# Educational and Vocational Counseling Services Provide Direction to Veterans

The Vocational Rehabilitation and Employment (VR&E) program provides educational and vocational counseling to servicemembers, veterans, and certain dependents (U.S.C. Title 38, Section 3697). These counseling services are designed to help an individual choose a vocational direction, determine the course needed to achieve the chosen goal, and evaluate the career possibilities open to them.

Assistance may include interest and aptitude testing, occupational exploration, setting occupational goals, locating the right type of training program, and exploring educational or training facilities which can be utilized to achieve an occupational goal.  Counseling services include, but are not limited to, educational and vocational counseling and guidance; testing; analysis of and recommendations to improve job marketing skills; identification of employment, training, and financial aid resources; and referrals to other agencies providing these services.

Eligibility for this service is based on having eligibility for a VA program such as Chapter 30 (Montgomery GI Bill); Chapter 31 (Vocational Rehabilitation and Employment); Chapter 32 (Veterans Education Assistance Program – VEAP); Chapter 35 (Dependents Education Assistance Program) for certain spouses and dependent children; Chapter 18 (Spina Bifida Program) for certain dependent children; and Chapter 106 and 107 of Title 10.

Educational and vocational counseling is available during the period the individual is on active duty with the armed forces and is within 180 days of the estimated date of his or her discharge or release from active duty.  The projected discharge must be under conditions other than dishonorable.  Servicemembers are eligible even if they are only considering whether or not they will continue as members of the armed forces.  Veterans are eligible if not more than one year has elapsed since the date the individual was last discharged or released from active duty.

Veterans and servicemembers may apply for the counseling ser-vices using VA Form 28-8832, Application for Counseling.  Veterans and servicemembers may also write a letter expressing a desire for counseling services.  Upon receipt of either type of request for counseling from an eligible individual, the VR&E Division will schedule an appointment for counseling.

Counseling services are provided to eligible persons at no charge.

## Veterans' Workforce Investment Program

Recently separated veterans and those with service-connected disabilities, significant barriers to employment or who served on active duty during a period in which a campaign or expedition badge was authorized can contact the nearest state employment office for employment help through the Veterans' Workforce Investment Program. The program may be conducted through state or local public agencies, community organizations or private, nonprofit organizations.

## State Employment Services

Veterans can find employment information, education and training opportunities, job counseling, job search workshops, and resume preparation assistance at state Workforce Career or One-Stop Centers. These offices also have specialists to help disabled veterans find employment.

## Veterans May be Eligible for Unemployment Compensation for a Limited Time Period

Veterans who do not begin civilian employment immediately after leaving military service may receive weekly unemployment compensation for a limited period of time. The amount and duration of payments are determined by individual states. Apply by contacting the nearest state employment office listed in your local telephone directory.

## Veterans Receive Preference When Applying for Federal Jobs

Since the time of the Civil War, veterans of the U.S. armed forces have been given some degree of preference in appointments to federal jobs.  Veterans' preference in its present form comes from the Veterans' Preference Act of 1944, as amended, and now codified in various provisions of Title 5, United States Code.  By law, veterans who are disabled or who served on active duty in the U.S. armed forces during certain specified time periods or in military campaigns are entitled to preference over others when hiring from competitive lists of eligible candidates, and also in retention during a reduction in force (RIF).

To receive preference, a veteran must have been discharged or released from active duty in the U.S. armed forces under honorable conditions (with an honorable or general discharge).  Preference is also provided for certain widows and widowers of deceased veterans who died in service; spouses of service-connected disabled veterans; and mothers of veterans who died under honorable conditions on active duty or have permanent and total service-connected disabilities.  This type of preference is referred to as "derived preference" because it is based on service of a veteran who is not able to use the preference.  For each of these preferences, there are specific criteria that must be met in order to be eligible to receive the veterans' preference.

Recent changes in Title 5 clarify veterans' preference eligibility criteria for National Guard and Reserve servicemembers.  Veterans eligible for preference now include National Guard and Reserve servicemembers who served on active duty as defined by Title 38 at any time in the armed forces for a period of more than 180 consecutive days, any part of which occurred during the period beginning on Sept. 11, 2001, and ending on the date prescribed by Presidential proclamation or by law as the last date of OIF.  The National Guard and Reserve servicemembers must have been discharged or released from active duty in the armed forces under honorable conditions.  These changes were effective Jan. 6, 2006.

Another recent change involves veterans who earned the Global War on Terrorism Expeditionary Medal for service in OEF.  Under Title 5, service on active duty in the armed forces during a war or in a campaign or expedition for which a campaign badge has been authorized also qualifies for veterans' preference.  Any Armed Forces Expeditionary medal or campaign badge qualifies for preference.  Medal holders must have served continuously for 24 months or the full period called or ordered to active duty.  As of December 2005, veterans who received the Global War on Terrorism Expeditionary Medal are entitled to veterans' preference if otherwise eligible.  For additional information on veterans' preference, visit the Office of Personnel Management (OPM) website at http://opm.gov/veterans/html/vetguide.asp#2.

Veterans' preference does not require an agency to use any particular appointment process.  Agencies can pick candidates from a number of different special hiring authorities or through a variety of different sources.  For example, the agency can reinstate a former federal employee, transfer someone from another agency, reassign someone from within the agency, make a selection under merit promotion procedures or through open, competitive exams, or appoint someone noncompetitively under special authority such as a Veterans Readjustment Appointment or special authority for 30 percent or more disabled veterans. The decision on which hiring authority the agency desires to use rests solely with the agency.

When applying for federal jobs, eligible veterans should claim preference on their application or resume.  Veterans should apply for a federal job by contacting the personnel office at the agency in which they wish to work. For more information, visit http://www.usajobs.opm.gov/ for job openings or help creating a federal resume.

**Veterans' Employment Opportunities Act:** When an agency accepts applications from outside its own workforce, the Veterans' Employment Opportunities Act (VEOA) of 1998 allows preference eligible candidates or veterans to compete for these vacancies under merit promotion procedures.  Veterans who are selected are given career or career-conditional appointments.  Veterans are those who have been separated under honorable conditions from the U.S. armed forces with three or more years of continuous active service. For information, visit http://www.usajobs.opm.gov/ei52.asp.

**Veterans' Recruitment Appointment:** Allows federal agencies to appoint eligible veterans to jobs without competition. These appointments can be converted to career or career-conditional positions after two years of satisfactory work. Veterans should apply directly to the agency where they wish to work. For information, visit http://www.usajobs.opm.gov/ei4.asp.

# Center for Veterans Enterprise Helps Veterans Form Small Businesses

VA's Center for Veterans Enterprise helps veterans interested in forming or expanding small businesses and helps VA contracting offices identify veteran-owned small businesses. For information, write the U.S. Department of Veterans Affairs (OOVE), 810 Vermont Avenue, N.W., Washington, DC 20420-0001, call toll-free 1-866-584-2344 or visit http://www.vetbiz.gov/.

**Small Business Contracts:** Like other federal agencies, VA is required to place a portion of its contracts and purchases with small and disadvantaged businesses. VA has a special office to help small and disadvantaged businesses get information on VA acquisition opportunities. For information, write the U.S. Department of Veterans Affairs (OOSB), 810 Vermont Avenue, N.W., Washington, DC 20420-0001, call toll-free 1-800-949-8387 or visit http://www.va.gov/osdbu/.

# *Chapter 11*

# Benefits for Dependents and Survivors

*Bereavement Counseling, VA Death Pension Eligibility and Payment Rates, Dependency and Indemnity Compensation Eligibility and Payment Rates, VA Provides Educational Assistance to Qualifying Dependents, VA Medical Care*

## VA Provides Bereavement Counseling to Family Members of Servicemembers

VA Vet Centers provide bereavement counseling to all family members including spouses, children, parents and siblings of servicemembers who die while on active duty. This includes federally activated members of the National Guard and reserve components. Bereavement services may be accessed by calling (202) 273-9116 or e-mail vet.center@va.gov.

## Death Pension

VA provides pensions to low-income surviving spouses and unmarried children of deceased veterans with wartime service.

**Eligibility:** To be eligible, spouses must not have remarried and children must be under age 18, or under age 23 if attending a VA-approved school, or have become permanently incapable of self-support because of disability before age 18.

The veteran must have been discharged under conditions other than dishonorable and must have had 90 days or more of active military service, at least one day of which was during a period of war, or a service-connected disability justifying discharge. Longer periods of service may be required for veterans who entered active duty on or after Sept. 8, 1980, or Oct. 16, 1981, if an officer. If the veteran died in service but not in the line of duty, the death pension may be payable if the veteran had completed at least two years of honorable service.

Children who become incapable of self-support because of a disability before age 18 may be eligible for the death pension as long as the condition exists, unless the child marries or the child's income exceeds the applicable limit.

A surviving spouse may be entitled to a higher income limit if living in a nursing home, in need of the aid and attendance of another person or is permanently housebound.

**Payment:** The death pension provides a monthly payment to bring an eligible person's income to a level established by law. The payment is reduced by the annual income from other sources such as Social Security. The payment may be increased if the recipient has unreimbursed medical expenses that can be deducted from countable income.

| 2007 VA Death Pension Rates<br>Paid to Veterans' Survivors | |
| --- | --- |
| **Recipient of Pension** | **Maximum Annual Rate** |
| Surviving spouse | $7,329 |
| (With dependent child) | $9,594 |
| Permanently housebound | $8,957 |
| (With dependent child) | $11,219 |
| In need of regular aid and attendance | $11,715 |
| (With dependent child) | $13,976 |
| For each additional dependent child | $1,866 |
| Pension for each surviving child | $1,866 |

# Military Services Provide Death Gratuity Payment to Servicemembers' Next of Kin

Military services provide payment, called a death gratuity, in the amount of $12,420 to the next of kin of servicemembers who die while on active duty or retirees who die within 120 days of retirement as a result of service-connected injury or illness. In cases where servicemembers die as a result of hostile actions in a designated combat operation or combat zone, or while training for combat or performing hazardous duty, military services pay $100,000 to the next of kin. Parents, brothers or sisters may be provided the payment, if designated as next of kin by the deceased. The payment is made by the last military command of the deceased. If the beneficiary is not paid automatically, application may be made to the military service concerned.

# Dependency and Indemnity Compensation

**Eligibility:** For a survivor to be eligible for Dependency and Indemnity Compensation (DIC), the veteran's death must have resulted from one of the following causes:

1. A disease or injury incurred or aggravated in the line of duty while on active duty or active duty for training.
2. An injury incurred or aggravated in the line of duty while on inactive duty training.
3. A service-connected disability or a condition directly related to a service-connected disability.

DIC also may be paid to survivors of veterans who were totally disabled from service-connected conditions at the time of death, even though their service-connected disabilities did not cause their deaths.

The survivor qualifies if the veteran was:

1. Continuously rated totally disabled for a period of 10 years immediately preceding death.
2. Continuously rated totally disabled from the date of military discharge and for at least five years immediately preceding death.
3. Or a former POW who died after Sept. 30, 1999, and who was continuously rated totally disabled for a period of at least one year immediately preceding death.

Payments will be offset by any amount received from judicial proceedings brought on by the veteran's death. The discharge must have been under conditions other than dishonorable.

**Payments for Deaths After Jan. 1, 1993:**  Surviving spouses of veterans who died on or after Jan. 1, 1993, receive a basic rate, plus additional payments for dependent children, for the aid and attendance of another person if they are patients in a nursing home or require the regular assistance of another person, or if they are permanently housebound.

| 2007 VA Death Payment Rates to Veterans'* Surviving Spouses | |
| --- | --- |
| **Allowances** | **Monthly Rate Paid to Surviving Spouse** |
| Basic Payment Rate | $1,067 |
| *Additional Allowances:* | |
| Each Dependent Child | $265 |
| Aid and Attendance | $265 |
| Housebound | $126 |

**Veterans who died on or after Jan. 1, 1993.*

**Special Allowances:** Add $228 if the veteran was totally disabled eight continuous years prior to death. Add $250 to the additional allowance for dependent children for the initial two years of entitlement for DIC awards commencing on or after Jan. 1, 2005.

**Payments for Deaths Prior to Jan. 1, 1993:** Surviving spouses of veterans who died prior to Jan. 1, 1993, receive an amount based on the deceased's military pay grade.

| 2007 VA Death Payment Rates Paid Monthly to Veterans'* Surviving Spouses | | | | | |
| --- | --- | --- | --- | --- | --- |
| Enlisted Pay Grade of Deceased | Rate Paid to Surviving Spouse | Warrant Officer Pay Grade of Deceased | Rate Paid to Surviving Spouse | Commissioned Officer Pay Grade of Deceased | Rate Paid to Surviving Spouse |
| E-1 | $1,067 | W-1 | $1,128 | O-1 | $1,128 |
| E-2 | $1,067 | W-2 | $1,172 | O-2 | $1,165 |
| E-3 | $1,067 | W-3 | $1,207 | O-3 | $1,246 |
| E-4 | $1,067 | W-4 | $1,276 | O-4 | $1,319 |
| E-5 | $1,067 | | | O-5 | $1,452 |
| E-6 | $1,067 | | | O-6 | $1,637 |
| E-7 | $1,104 | | | O-7 | $1,768 |
| E-8 | $1,165 | | | O-8 | $1,941 |
| E-9 | $1,215 | | | O-9 | $2,076 |
| | | | | O-10 | $2,276 |

**Veterans who died prior to Jan. 1, 1993.*

**Payments to Parents:** The monthly payment for parents of deceased veterans depends upon their income.

**Restored Entitlement Program for Survivors:** Survivors of veterans who died of service-connected causes incurred or aggravated prior to Aug. 13, 1981, may be eligible for a special benefit payable in addition to any other benefits to which the family may be entitled. The amount of the benefit is based on information provided by the Social Security Administration.

# VA Provides Educational Assistance to Qualifying Dependents of Veterans

**Eligibility:** VA provides educational assistance to qualifying dependents as follows:

1. The spouse or child of a servicemember who either died of a  service-connected disability, or who has permanent and total service-connected disability, or who died while such a disability existed.

2. The spouse or child of a servicemember listed for more than 90 days as currently Missing in Action (MIA), captured in the line of duty by a hostile force, or detained or interned by a foreign government or power.

3. The spouse or child of a servicemember who is hospitalized or is receiving outpatient care or treatment for a disability that is determined to be totally and permanently disabling, incurred or aggravated due to active duty, and for which the service member is likely to be discharged.

Surviving spouses lose eligibility if they remarry before age 57 or are living with another person who has been held out publicly as their spouse.  They can regain eligibility if their remarriage ends by death or divorce or if they cease living with the person. Dependent children do not lose eligibility if the surviving spouse remarries. Visit www.gibill.va.gov/ for more information.

**Period of Eligibility:** The period of eligibility for veterans' spouses expires 10 years from the date they become eligible or the date of the veteran's death. VA may grant an extension. Children generally must be between the ages of 18 and 26 to receive educational benefits, though extensions may be granted.

The period of eligibility for spouses of servicemembers who died on active duty expires 20 years from the date of death. This is a change in law that became effective Dec. 10, 2004. Spouses of servicemembers who died on active duty whose 10-year eligibility period expired before Dec. 10, 2004, now have 20 years from the date of death to use educational benefits.

**Payments:** The payment rate effective Oct. 1, 2006, is $860 a month for full-time school attendance, with lesser amounts for part time. Benefits are paid for full-time training for up to 45 months or the equivalent in part-time training.

**Training Available:** Benefits may be awarded for pursuit of associate, bachelor or graduate degrees at colleges and universities, independent study, cooperative training, study abroad, certificate or diploma from business, technical or vocational schools, apprenticeships, on-the-job training programs and farm cooperative courses. Benefits for correspondence courses under certain conditions are available to spouses only.

Beneficiaries without high-school degrees can pursue secondary schooling, and those with a deficiency in a subject may receive tutorial assistance if enrolled halftime or more.

**Work-Study:** Participants who train at the three-quarter or full-time rate may be eligible for a work-study program in which they work for VA and receive hourly wages. The types of work allowed include:

1. Outreach services.
2. VA paperwork.
3. Work at national or state veterans cemeteries.
4. Work at VA medical centers or state veterans homes.
5. Other VA approved activities.

**Counseling:** VA may provide counseling to help participants pursue an educational or vocational objective.

**Special Benefits:** Dependents over age 14 with physical or mental disabilities that impair their ability to pursue an education may receive specialized vocational or restorative training, including speech and voice correction, language retraining, lip reading, auditory training, Braille reading and writing, and similar programs. Certain disabled or surviving spouses are also eligible for vocational or restorative training.

**Montgomery GI Bill Death Benefit:** VA will pay a special Montgomery GI Bill death benefit to a designated survivor in the event of the service-connected death of a servicemember while on active duty or within one year after discharge or release.

The deceased must either have been entitled to educational assistance under the Montgomery GI Bill program or a participant in the program who would have been so entitled but for the high school diploma or length-of-service requirement. The amount paid will be equal to the participant's actual military pay reduction, less any education benefits paid.

# VA Medical Care Provided to Family Members

The Civilian Health and Medical Program of VA (CHAMPVA), provides reimbursement for most medical expenses – inpatient, outpatient, mental health, prescription medication, skilled nursing care and durable medical equipment.

**Eligibility:** To be eligible for CHAMPVA, an individual cannot be eligible for TRICARE (the medical program for civilian dependents provided by DOD) and must be one of the following:

1. The spouse or child of a veteran who VA has rated permanently and totally disabled for a service-connected disability.

2. The surviving spouse or child of a veteran who died from a VA-rated service-connected disability, or who, at the time of death, was rated permanently and totally disabled.

3. The surviving spouse or child of a servicemember who died in the line of duty, not due to misconduct. However, in most of these cases, these family members are eligible for TRICARE, not CHAMPVA.

A surviving spouse under age 55 who remarries loses CHAMPVA eligibility on midnight of the date of remarriage. However, they may re-establish eligibility if the remarriage ends by death, divorce or annulment effective the first day of the month following the termination of the remarriage or Dec. 1, 1999, whichever is later. A surviving spouse who remarries after age 55 does not lose eligibility upon remarriage.

Those with Medicare entitlement may also have CHAMPVA eligibility secondary to Medicare. Eligibility limitations apply. For additional information, contact the VA Health Administration Center, P.O. Box 65023, Denver, CO 80206, call 1-800-733-8387 or visit the website at http://www.va.gov/hac/hacmain.asp.

Many VA medical centers provide services to CHAMPVA beneficiaries under the CHAMPVA In House Treatment Initiative (CITI) program.

Contact the nearest VA medical center to determine if it participates. Those who use a CITI facility incur no cost for services; however, services are provided on a space available basis, after the needs of veterans are met. Not all services are available at all times. CHAMP-VA beneficiaries covered by Medicare cannot use CITI.

# Children of Veterans Born with Birth Defects

Children of Vietnam veterans born with certain birth defects may be eligible for a monthly monetary allowance, health care specific to the disability, and vocational training if reasonably feasible.

The law defines "child" as the natural child of a Vietnam veteran, regardless of age or marital status. The child must have been conceived after the date on which the veteran first entered the Republic of Vietnam.  For more information about benefits for children with birth defects, visit www.va.gov/hac/forbeneficiaries/spina/spina.asp.

**Children of Vietnam or Korean Veterans Born with Spina Bifida:**
Biological children of male and female veterans who served in Vietnam at any time during the period beginning Jan. 9, 1962, and ending May 7, 1975, or who served in or near the Korean demilitarized zone (DMZ) during the period beginning Sept. 1, 1967, and ending Aug. 31, 1971, may be eligible for certain benefits.

A monetary allowance is paid at one of three disability levels based on the neurological manifestations that define the severity of disability: impairment of the functioning of extremities, impairment of bowel or bladder function, and impairment of intellectual functioning.

| 2007 VA Benefits for Children of Vietnam or Korean Veterans Born with Certain Birth Defects | | | |
| --- | --- | --- | --- |
| | Disability Level I | Disability Level II | Disability Level III |
| Monthly Rate* | $263 | $909 | $1,550 |

** Effective Dec. 1, 2006*

**Children of Women Vietnam Veterans Born with Certain Birth Defects:** Biological children of women veterans who served in Vietnam at any time during the period beginning on Feb. 28, 1961, and ending on May 7, 1975, may be eligible for certain benefits because of birth defects associated with the mother's service in Vietnam that resulted in a permanent physical or mental disability. The covered birth defects do not include conditions due to family disorders, birth-related injuries, or fetal or neonatal infirmities with well-established causes.

A monetary allowance is paid at one of four disability levels based on the child's degree of permanent disability.

| 2007 VA Benefits for Children of Women Vietnam Veterans Born with Certain Birth Defects | | | | |
| --- | --- | --- | --- | --- |
| | Disability Level I | Disability Level II | Disability Level III | Disability Level IV |
| Monthly Rate* | $120 | $263 | $909 | $1,550 |

** Effective Dec. 1, 2006*

**Vocational Training:** VA provides vocational counseling, rehabilitation, education and training to help these children prepare for and attain suitable employment.

To qualify, an applicant must be a child with a VA monthly allowance for spina bifida or another covered birth defect and for whom VA has determined that achievement of a vocational goal is reasonably feasible. A child may not begin vocational training before their 18th birthday or the date they complete secondary schooling, whichever comes first. Depending on need and eligibility, a child may be provided up to 48 months of full-time training.

## VA Home Loan Guaranty May be Available to Veterans' Spouses

A VA loan guaranty to acquire a home may be available to an unmarried spouse of a veteran or servicemember who died as a result of service-connected disabilities, a surviving spouse who remarries after age 57, or to a spouse of a servicemember officially listed as MIA or who is currently a POW for more than 90 days. Spouses of those listed MIA/POW are limited to one loan.

## "No-Fee" Passports Available to Family Members Visiting Overseas Cemeteries

"No-fee" passports are available for family members visiting graves or memorial sites at World War I and World War II overseas American military cemeteries. Eligibility is limited to surviving spouses, parents, children, sisters, brothers and guardians of the deceased who are buried or commemorated in American military cemeteries on foreign soil.

For additional information, write: American Battle Monuments Commission, Courthouse Plaza II, Suite 500, 2300 Clarendon Blvd., Arlington, VA  22201, call 703-696-6900, or visit http://www.abmc.gov/home.php.

# *Chapter 12*

# Appeals of VA Claims Decisions

*Board of Veterans' Appeals Makes Decisions on Appeals, U.S. Court of Appeals for Veterans Claims Offers Independent Review*

Veterans and other claimants for VA benefits have the right to appeal decisions made by a VA regional office or medical center. Typical issues appealed are disability compensation, pension, education benefits, recovery of overpayments, and reimbursement for unauthorized medical services.

A claimant has one year from the date of the notification of a VA decision to file an appeal. The first step in the appeal process is for a claimant to file a written notice of disagreement with the VA regional office or medical center that made the decision.

Following receipt of the written notice, VA will furnish the claimant a "Statement of the Case" describing what facts, laws and regulations were used in deciding the case. To complete the request for appeal, the claimant must file a "Substantive Appeal" within 60 days of the mailing of the Statement of the Case, or within one year from the date VA mailed its decision, whichever period ends later.

## Board of Veterans' Appeals Makes Decisions on Appeals on Behalf of VA Secretary

The Board of Veterans' Appeals makes decisions on appeals on behalf of the Secretary of Veterans Affairs. Although it is not required, a veterans' service organization, an agent or an attorney may represent a claimant. Appellants may present their cases in person to a member of the Board at a hearing in Washington, D.C., at a VA regional office or by videoconference.

Decisions made by the Board can be found on the website at http://www.va.gov/vbs/bva/. The  pamphlet, "Understanding the Appeal Process," is available on the website or may be requested by writing: Hearings and Transcription Unit (0141A), Board of Veterans' Appeals, 810 Vermont Avenue, NW, Washington, DC 20420.

## U.S. Court of Appeals for Veterans Claims Offers Independent Review

A final Board of Veterans' Appeals decision that does not grant a claimant the benefits desired may be appealed to the U.S. Court of Appeals for Veterans Claims, an independent court, not part of the Department of Veterans Affairs.

Notice of an appeal must be received by the court with a postmark that is within 120 days after the Board of Veterans' Appeals mailed its decision. The court reviews the record considered by the Board of Veterans' Appeals. It does not hold trials or receive new evidence.

Appellants may represent themselves before the court or have lawyers or approved agents as representatives. Oral argument is held only at the direction of the court. Either party may appeal a decision of the court to the U.S. Court of Appeals for the Federal Circuit and may seek review in the Supreme Court of the United States.

Published decisions, case status information, rules and procedures, and other special announcements can be found on the court's website at http://www.vetapp.gov/. The court's decisions can also be found in West's Veterans Appeals Reporter, and on the Westlaw and LEXIS online services. For questions, write the Clerk of the Court, 625 Indiana Ave. NW, Suite 900, Washington, DC 20004, or call (202) 501-5970.

# Chapter 13
## Military Medals and Records

*Process for Replacing Military Medals, Process for Replacing Military Records, Requests for Correction of Military Records Must be Filed Within Three Years, Process for Applying for a Review of Discharge*

## Process For Replacing Military Medals

Medals awarded while in active service are issued by the individual military services if requested by veterans or their next of kin. Requests for replacement medals, decorations, and awards should be directed to the branch of the military in which the veteran served. However, for Air Force (including Army Air Corps) and Army veterans, the National Personnel Records Center (NPRC) verifies awards and forwards requests and verification to appropriate services.

Requests for replacement medals should be submitted on Standard Form 180, "Request Pertaining To Military Records," which may be obtained at VA offices or the Internet at http://www.va.gov/vaforms/. Forms, addresses, and other information on requesting medals can be found on the Military Personnel Records section of NPRC's website at htttp://www.archives.gov/st-louis/military-personnel/index.html. For questions, call Military Personnel Records at (314) 801-0800 or e-mail questions to: MPR.center@nara.gov.

When requesting medals, type or clearly print the veteran's full name, include the veteran's branch of service, service number or Social Security number and provide the veteran's exact or approximate dates of military service. The request must contain the signature of the veteran or next of kin if the veteran is deceased. If available, include a copy of the discharge or separation document, WDAGO Form 53-55 or DD Form 214.

## Process For Replacing Military Records

If discharge or separation documents are lost, veterans or the next of kin of deceased veterans may obtain duplicate copies by completing forms found on the Internet at http://www.archives.gov/research/index.html and mailing or faxing them to the NPRC.

Alternatively, write the National Personnel Records Center, Military Personnel Records, 9700 Page Blvd., St. Louis, MO 63132-5100. Specify that a duplicate separation document is needed. The veteran's full name should be printed or typed so that it can be read clearly, but the request must also contain the signature of the veteran or the signature of the next of kin, if the veteran is deceased. Include the veteran's branch of service, service number or Social Security number and exact or approximate dates and years of service. Use Standard Form 180, "Request Pertaining To Military Records."

It is not necessary to request a duplicate copy of a veteran's discharge or separation papers solely for the purpose of filing a claim for VA benefits. If complete information about the veteran's service is furnished on the application, VA will obtain verification of service.

## Requests for Correction of Military Records Must be Filed Within Three Years

The secretary of a military department, acting through a Board for Correction of Military Records, has authority to change any military record when necessary to correct an error or remove an injustice. A correction board may consider applications for correction of a military record, including a review of a discharge issued by courts martial.

The veteran, survivor or legal representative must file a request for correction within three years after discovering an alleged error or injustice. The board may excuse failure to file within this time, however, if it finds it would be in the interest of justice. It is an applicant's responsibility to show why the filing of the application was delayed and why it would be in the interest of justice for the board to consider it despite the delay.

To justify a correction, it is necessary to show to the satisfaction of the board that the alleged entry or omission in the records was in error or unjust. Applications should include all available evidence, such as signed statements of witnesses or a brief of arguments supporting the correction. Application is made with DD Form 149, available at VA offices, veterans organizations or visit http://www.dtic.mil/whs/directives/infomgt/forms/formsprogram.htm.

## Process for Applying for Review of Veteran's Discharge from Military Service

Each of the military services maintains a discharge review board with authority to change, correct or modify discharges or dismissals not issued by a sentence of a general courts-martial. The board has no authority to address medical discharges.

The veteran or, if the veteran is deceased or incompetent, the surviving spouse, next of kin or legal representative may apply for a review of discharge by writing to the military department concerned, using DD Form 293 -- "Application for the Review of Discharge from the Armed Forces of the United States." This form may be obtained at a VA regional office, from veterans organizations or from the Internet at http://www.dtic.mil/whs/directives/infomgt/forms/formsprogram.htm.

However, if the discharge was more than 15 years ago, a veteran must petition the appropriate service Board for Correction of Military Records using DD Form 149 -- "Application for Correction of Military Records Under the Provisions of Title 10, U.S. Code, Section 1552." A discharge review is conducted by a review of an applicant's record and, if requested, by a hearing before the board.

Discharges awarded as a result of a continuous period of unauthorized absence in excess of 180 days make persons ineligible for VA benefits regardless of action taken by discharge review boards, unless VA determines there were compelling circumstances for the absence. Boards for the Correction of Military Records also may consider such cases.

Veterans with disabilities incurred or aggravated during active duty may qualify for medical or related benefits regardless of separation and characterization of service. Veterans separated administratively under other than honorable conditions may request that their discharge be reviewed for possible recharacterization, provided they file their appeal within 15 years of the date of separation.

Questions regarding the review of a discharge should be addressed to the appropriate discharge review board at the address listed on DOD Form 293.

# Chapter 14
# Benefits Provided by Other Federal Agencies

*USDA Provides Loans for Farms and Homes, Housing and Urban Development Veteran Resource Center, Small Business Administration Conducts Outreach to Veterans, Social Security Benefits, Commissary and Exchange Privileges for Veterans and Family Members*

## USDA Provides Loans for Farms and Homes

The U.S. Department of Agriculture (USDA) provides loans and guarantees to buy, improve or operate farms. Loans and guarantees are available for housing in towns generally up to 20,000 in population. Applications from veterans have preference. For further information, contact Farm Service Agency or Rural Development, USDA, 1400 Independence Ave., S.W., Washington, DC 20250, or apply at local Department of Agriculture offices, usually located in county seats.

## Housing and Urban Development Veteran Resource Center (HUDVET)

Housing and Urban Development (HUD) sponsors the Veteran Resource Center (HUDVET), which works with national veterans service organizations to serve as a general information center on all HUD sponsored housing and community development programs and services. To contact HUDVET, call 1-800-998-9999, TDD 800-483-2209, or visit their website at http://www.hud.gov/hudvet.

# Veterans Receive Naturalization Preference

Honorable active-duty service in the U.S. armed forces during a designated period of hostility allows an individual to naturalize without being required to establish any periods of residence or physical presence in the United States.  A servicemember who was in the United States, certain territories, or aboard an American public vessel at the time of enlistment, re-enlistment, extension of enlistment or induction, may naturalize even if he or she is not a lawful permanent resident.

On July 3, 2002, the president issued Executive Order 13269 establishing a new period of hostility for naturalization purposes beginning Sept. 11, 2001, and continuing until a date designated by a future Executive Order.  Qualifying members of the armed forces who have served at any time during a specified period of hostility may immediately apply for naturalization using the current application – Form N-400 -- "Application for Naturalization."  Additional information about filing and requirement fees and designated period of hostility are available on the U.S. Citizenship and Immigration Services (USCIS) website at www.uscis.gov.

Individuals who served honorably in the U.S. armed forces, but were no longer serving on active duty status as of Sept. 11, 2001, may still be naturalized without having to comply with the residence and physical presence requirements for naturalization if they filed Form N-400 while still serving in the U.S. armed forces or within six months of termination of their active duty service.  An individual who files the application for naturalization after the six-month period following termination of active-duty service is not exempt from the residence and physical presence requirements, but can count any period of active-duty service towards the residence and physical presence requirements.  Individuals seeking naturalization under this provision must establish that they are lawful permanent residents (such status not having been lost, rescinded or abandoned) and that they served honorably in the U.S. armed forces for at least one year.

If a servicemember dies as a result of injury or disease incurred or aggravated by service during a time of combat, the servicemember's survivor(s) can apply for the deceased servicemember to receive posthumous citizenship at any time within two years of the servicemember's death. The issuance of a posthumous certificate of citizenship does not confer U.S. citizenship on surviving relatives. However, a non-U.S. citizen spouse or qualifying family member may file for certain immigration benefits and services based upon their relationship to a servicemember who died during hostilities or a non-citizen servicemember who died during hostilities and was later granted posthumous citizenship.  For additional information, visit the USCIS website at www.uscis.gov.

## Small Business Administration (SBA) Conducts Outreach to Veterans

The U.S. Small Business Administration's Office of Veterans Business Development conducts comprehensive outreach to veterans, service-disabled veterans, and Reserve Component members of the U.S. military.  In addition, the office is the source for the formulation, execution, and promotion of policies and programs of the Small Business Administration (SBA) that provide assistance to veteran-owned small businesses. SBA is the primary federal agency responsible for assisting veterans who own or are considering starting small businesses.

Among the services provided are business counseling and training through five Veterans Business Outreach Centers, more than 1,000 Small Business Development Centers, nearly 400 SCORE Chapters with 11,000 volunteer counselors, 100 Women Business Centers, as well as various loan and loan guarantee programs ranging from micro loans to venture capital assistance.  Veterans participate in all SBA federal procurement programs, and the SBA supports veterans and others in international trade.

A special Military Reservist Economic Injury Disaster Loan is available for self-employed Reservists whose small businesses may have been damaged through extended absences of the owner or essential employee as a result of activation of the owner or essential employee to military active duty. The SBA also conducts important research in veterans' entrepreneurship.  A Veterans Business Development Officer is stationed at every SBA District Office.  Information about SBA's full range of services can be found at http://www.sba.gov/vets/ and for Reservists at www.sba.gov/reservists/, or by calling 202-205-6773 or 1-800-U-ASK-SBA (1-800-827-5722).

# Social Security Administration Provides Benefits to Veterans and Dependents

Monthly retirement, disability and survivor benefits under Social Security are payable to veterans and dependents if the veteran has earned enough work credits under the program. Upon the veteran's death, a one-time payment of $255 also may be made to the veteran's spouse or child. In addition, a veteran may qualify at age 65 for Medicare's hospital insurance and medical insurance. Medicare protection is available to people who have received Social Security disability benefits for 24 months, and to insured people and their dependents who need dialysis or kidney transplants, or who have amyotrophic lateral sclerosis (more commonly known as Lou Gehrig's disease).

Since 1957, military service earnings for active duty (including active duty for training) have counted toward Social Security and those earnings are already on Social Security records. Since 1988, inactive duty service in the Reserve Component (such as weekend drills) has also been covered by Social Security. Servicemembers and veterans are credited with $300 credit in additional earnings for each calendar quarter in which they received active duty basic pay after 1956 and before 1978.

Veterans who served in the military from 1978 through 2001 are credited with an additional $100 in earnings for each $300 in active duty basic pay, up to a maximum of $1,200 a year. No additional Social Security taxes are withheld from pay for these extra credits.  If veterans enlisted after Sept. 7, 1980, and did not complete at least 24 months of active duty or their full tour of duty, they may not be able to receive the additional earnings.  Check with Social Security for details.  Additional earnings will no longer be credited for military service periods after 2001.

Also, noncontributory Social Security earnings of $160 a month may be credited to veterans who served after Sept. 15, 1940, and before 1957, including attendance at service academies. For information, call 1-800-772-1213 or visit http://www.socialsecurity.gov/.  (Note: Social Security cannot add these extra earnings to the record until an application is filed for Social Security benefits.)

# Eligibility for Monthly Supplemental Security Income (SSI)

Those age 65 or older and those who are blind or otherwise disabled may be eligible for monthly Supplemental Security Income (SSI) payments if they have little or no income or resources. States may supplement the federal payments to eligible persons and may disregard additional income.

Although VA compensation and pension benefits are counted in determining income for SSI purposes, some other income is not counted. Also, not all resources count in determining eligibility. For example, a person's home and the land it is on do not count. Personal effects, household goods, automobiles and life insurance may not count, depending upon their value. Information and help is available at any Social Security office or by calling 1-800-772-1213.

# Eligibility for Living in the Armed Forces Retirement Home in Washington, D.C.

Veterans are eligible to live in the Armed Forces Retirement Home located in Washington, D.C., if their active duty military service is at least 50 percent enlisted, warrant officer or limited duty officer if they qualify under one of the following categories:

1. Are 60 years of age or older; and were discharged or released under honorable conditions after 20 or more years of active service.
2. Are determined to be incapable of earning a livelihood because of a service-connected disability incurred in the line of duty.
3. Served in a war theater during a time of war declared by Congress or were eligible for hostile fire special pay and were discharged or released under honorable conditions; and are determined to be incapable of earning a livelihood because of injuries, disease or disability.
4. Served in a women's component of the armed forces before June 12, 1948; and are determined to be eligible for admission due to compelling personal circumstances.

Eligibility determinations are based on rules prescribed by the Home's Chief Operating Officer. Veterans are not eligible if they have been convicted of a felony or are not free from alcohol, drug or psychiatric problems. Married couples are welcome, but both must be eligible in their own right. At the time of admission, applicants must be capable of living independently.

The Armed Forces Retirement Home is an independent federal agency. For information, call 1-800-332-3527 or 1-800-422-9988, or visit their website at http://www.afrh.gov/.

## Commissary and Exchange Privileges for Veterans and Family Members

Unlimited exchange and commissary store privileges in the United States are available to honorably discharged veterans with a service-connected disability rated at 100 percent, unremarried surviving spouses of members or retired members of the armed forces, recipients of the Medal of Honor, and their dependents and orphans. Certification of total disability is done by VA. Reservists and their dependents also may be eligible. Privileges overseas are governed by international law and are available only if agreed upon by the foreign government concerned.

Though these benefits are provided by DOD, VA does provide assistance in completing DD Form 1172, "Application for Uniformed Services Identification and Privilege Card." For detailed information, contact the nearest military installation.

# VA Facilities

Patients should call the telephone numbers listed to obtain clinic hours of operation and services. The following symbols indicate additional programs are available at medical centers:

* for nursing-home care units
# for domiciliaries

The following acronyms are used to indicate the specific type of clinic or site:

DC – Dental Clinic
MHC – Mental Health Clinic
OSAC – Outpatient Substance Abuse Clinic
OSP – Opiate Substitution Program
PTSD – Post Traumatic Stress Disorder Residential
    Rehabilitation Program
TWS – Therapeutic Work Site

Under the National Cemeteries listings, the acronym NC is used after the name of the town to designate locations of national cemeteries.

Please send address and telephone number corrections to:

Federal Benefits for Veterans and Dependents (80D)
810 Vermont Ave. NW
Washington, DC 20420

## ALABAMA
### Medical Centers:
Central AL Veterans Health Care System (1-800-214-8387):
    Montgomery 36109 (215 Perry Hill Rd., 334-272-4670)
    #*Tuskegee 36083 (2400 Hospital Rd., 334-727-0550)
Birmingham 35233 (700 S. 19th St., 205-933-8101)
*Tuscaloosa 35404 (3701 Loop Rd. East, 205-554-2000)

***Clinics:***
Anniston/Oxford 36203 (96 Ali Way, Creekside South, Oxford,
    256-832-4141)
Decatur/Madison 35758 (8075 Madison Blvd., Suite 101, Madison,
    256-772-6220)
Dothan 36301 (2020 Alexander Dr., 334-673-4166)
Dothan MHC 36301 (3753 Ross Clark Cir., Suite 4, 334-678-1903)
Florence Shoals Area Clinic 35660 (422 DD Cox Blvd.,
    256-381-9055)
Gadsden 35906 (206 Rescia Ave., 256-413-7154)
Huntsville 35801 (301 Governor's Dr., S.W., 256-535-3100)
Jasper 35501 (3400 Hwy 78 East, Medical Towers Suite 215,
    205-221-7384)
Mobile 36604 (1504 Springhill Ave., 251-219-3900)
***Regional Office:***
Montgomery 36109 (345 Perry Hill Rd., statewide 1-800-827-1000)
***Vet Centers:***
Birmingham 35233 (1500 5th Ave. S., 205-731-0550)
Mobile 36606 (2577 Government Blvd., 251-478-5906)
***National Cemeteries:***
Fort Mitchell NC 36856 (553 Hwy. 165, Seale, 334-855-4731)
Mobile NC 36604 (1202 Virginia St., 850-453-4846)

# ALASKA
***Medical Center:***
Alaska VA Healthcare System and Regional Office:
    Anchorage 99508-2989 (2925 DeBarr Rd, 907-257-4700)
    #Homeless Veterans Service: Anchorage 99503 (3001 C St.,
    1-800-764-2995)
***Clinics:***
Fairbanks 99703 (Ft. Wainwright, Bassett Army Hospital, Gaffney
    Rd., Bldg. 4065, Rm. 169/176, 907-353-6370)
Kenai 99611 (805 Frontage Rd., Suite 130, 907-283-2231 or
    1-877-797-8924)
***Regional Office:***
Anchorage 99508-2989 (2925 De Barr Rd., statewide
    1-800-827-1000)
***Benefits Office:***
Juneau 99802 (P.O. Box 20069, 907-586-7472)
***Vet Centers:***
Anchorage 99508 (4201 Tudor Centre Dr., Suite 115, 907-563-6966)

Fairbanks 99701 (540 4th Ave., Suite 100, 907-456-4238)
Kenai 99669 (Red Diamond Ctr., Bldg. F, Suite 4, 43335 Kalifornsky
    Beach Rd., 907-260-7640)
Wasilla 99654 (851 E. West Point Dr., Suite 111, 907-376-4318)
**National Cemeteries:**
Fort Richardson NC 99505-5498 (Building 997, Davis Highway,
    907-384-7075)
Sitka NC 99835 (803 Sawmill Creek Rd., 907-384-7075)

# AMERICAN SAMOA
**Benefits Office:**
Pago Pago 96799 (PO Box 1005, 684-633-5073)

# ARIZONA
**Medical Centers:**
*Phoenix 85012 (650 East Indian School Rd., 602-277-5551,
    Enrollment Ext. 6508, or 1-888-214-7264)
*#Prescott 86313 (500 Hwy. 89 North, 928-445-4860 or
    1-800-949-1005)
*Tucson 85723 (3601 S. 6th Ave., 520-792-1450 or 1-800-470-8262)
**Clinics:**
Anthem 85086 (3618 W. Anthem Way, Bldg., 120D, 928-445-4860
    extension 7200 or 623-551-6092)
Bellemont 86015 (Camp Navajo Army Depot, P.O. Box 16196,
    928-445-4860 extension 7820 or 928-226-1056)
Buckeye 85326 (1209 N. Miller Rd., 623-386-5785)
Casa Grande 85222 (Plaza del Sol, 900 E. Florence Blvd., Suites
    H&I, 520-629-4900 or 1-800-470-8262)
Cottonwood 86326 (203 Candy Ln., Suite 5B, 928-649-1532)
Globe 85501 (707 S. Broad St., 928-425-0027)
Green Valley 85615 (380 W. Vista Hermosa, Suite 140,
    520-629-4900 or 1-800-470-8262)
Kingman 86401 (1726 Beverly Ave., 928-445-4860 extension 6830
    or 928-692-0080)
Lake Havasu City 86403 (2035 Mesquite Ave., Southeast,
    928-445-4860 extension 7300 or 928-680-0090)
Mesa 85212 (6950 E. Williams Field Rd., 602-222-6568 ext. 3311)
Mena 71953 (1706 Hwy. 71 N, 479-394-4800)
Payson 85541 (1106 N. Beeline Hwy., 928-472-3148)
Safford 85546 (Bureau of Land Management., 711 S. 14th Ave.,
    520-629-4900 or 1-800-470-8262)

Show Low 85901 (2450 Show Low Lake Rd., Suites 1 & 3,
      928-532-1069)
Sierra Vista 85613 (Ft. Huachuca, Bliss Army Health Center, Bldg.
            45001, 520-629-4900 or 1-800-470-8262)
Sun City 85351 (10147W Grand Ave., Suite C, 602-222-2630,
      extension 3732)
Yuma 85365 (Bureau of Land Mgmt., 2555 E. Gila Ridge Rd.,
      520-629-4900 or 1-800-470-8262)
***Regional Office:***
Phoenix 85012 (3333 N. Central Ave., statewide 1-800-827-1000)
***Vet Centers:***
Phoenix 85012 (77 E. Weldon Ave., Suite 100, 602-640-2981)
Prescott 86303 (161 S. Granite St., Suite B, 928-778-3469)
Tucson 85719 (3055 N. 1st Ave., 520-882-0333)
***National Cemeteries:***
Nat. Mem. Cem. of AZ 85024 (23029 N. Cave Creek Rd., Phoenix,
      480-513-3600)
Prescott NC 86301 (500 Hwy. 89 N., 480-513-3600)


# ARKANSAS
***Medical Centers:***
Fayetteville 72703 (1100 N. College Ave., 479-443-4301)
Central Arkansas Veterans Healthcare System
      #*North Little Rock 72114 (2200 Fort Roots Dr., 501-257-1000)
      Little Rock 72205 (4300 W. 7th St., 501-257-1000)


***Clinics:***
El Dorado 71730 (460 West Oak, 870-862-2489)
Ft. Smith 72917 (Sparks Medical Plaza, 1500 Dodson Ave.,
      479-709-6850)
Harrison 72601 (Main St. Clinic, 707 N. Main St., 870-741-3592)
Hot Springs 71913 (1661 Airport Rd., Suite B, 501-760-1513)
Jonesboro 72401 (223 East Jackson, 870-972-0063)
Mountain Home 72653 (405 Buttercup Dr., 870-425-3030)
Paragould 72450 (1101 West Morgan, Suite 9, 870-236-9756)
Texarkana 71854 (910 Realtor Ave., 870-216-2242)
***Regional Office:***
North Little Rock 72114 (2200 Fort Roots Dr., Bldg. 65, statewide
      1-800-827-1000)
***Vet Center:***
North Little Rock 72114 (201 W. Broadway, Suite A, 501-324-6395)

### National Cemeteries:
Fayetteville NC 72701 (700 Government Ave., 479-444-5051)
Fort Smith NC 72901 (522 Garland Ave., 479-783-5345)
Little Rock NC 72206 (2523 Confederate Blvd., 501-324-6401)

## CALIFORNIA
### Medical Centers:
*Fresno 93703 (2615 E. Clinton Ave., 559-225-6100)
Greater Los Angeles Health Care System:
   #*West Los Angeles 90073 (11301 Wilshire Blvd., 310-478-3711)
Loma Linda Health Care System:
   * Loma Linda 92357 (11201 Benton St., 909-825-7084 or
1-800-741-8387)
Long Beach Health Care System:
   *Long Beach 90822 (5901 E. 7th St., 562-826-8000)
Northern California Health Care System:
   *Martinez 94553 (150 Muir Rd., 925-372-2000)
   Sacramento 95655 (10535 Hospital Way, 916-843-7000)
Palo Alto Health Care System:
   *Livermore 94550 (4951 Arroyo Rd., 925-373-4700)
   #*Menlo Park 94025 (795 Willow Rd., 650-493-5000)
   Palo Alto 94304 (3801 Miranda Ave., 650-493-5000)
San Diego Health Care System:
   *San Diego 92161 (3350 La Jolla Village Dr., 858-552-8585)
   *San Francisco 94121 (4150 Clement St., 415-221-4810)
### Clinics:
Anaheim 92801 (1801 W. Romneya Dr., Suite 303, 714-780-5400)
Antelope Valley/Lancaster 93536 (547 W. Lancaster Blvd.,
661-729-8655)
Atwater 95301 (3605 Hospital Rd., Suite D, 209-381-0105)
Auburn 95603 (11985 Heritage Oaks Pl., 1-888-227-5404)
Bakersfield 93301 (1801 Westwind Dr., 661-632-1800)
Cabrillo/Long Beach 90810 (2001 River Ave., Bldg. 28, Long Beach,
562-388-8000)
Capitola 95010 (At Santa Cruz Vet Center, 1350 N. 41st St., Suite
102, 831-464-5519)
Chico 95926 (280 Cohasset Rd., Suite 101, 530-879-5000)
Chula Vista 91910 (835 Third Ave., 619-409-1600)
Corona 92879 (800 Magnolia Ave, Suite 101, 951-817-8820)
East Los Angeles 90040 (5400 E. Olympic Blvd., 150, City of
Commerce, 323-725-7557)

Escondido 92025 (815 East Pennsylvania Ave., 760-466-7020)
Eureka 95501 (714 F St., 707-442-5335)
Fairfield 94535 (103 Bodin Cir., Building 778, Travis AFB,
    707-437-1800)
Gardena 90247 (1251 Redondo Beach Blvd., 3rd Fl., 310-851-4705)
Imperial Valley 92227 (528 G. St., Brawley, 760-344-9085)
Los Angeles 90012 (351 E. Temple St., 213-253-2677)
Mare Island 94592 (201 Walnut Ave., 707-562-8200)
*Martinez 94553 (150 Muir Rd., 925-372-2000)
McClellan 95652 (5342 Dudley Blvd., 916-561-7400)
McClellan 95652 (5401 Arnold Ave., 916-561-7800 or
    1-800-382-8387)
Mission Valley 92108 (8810 Rio San Diego Dr., 619-400-5000)
Modesto 95350 (1524 McHenry, Suite 315, 209-557-6200)
Monterey 93955 (located at Fort Ord, 3401 Engineer Lane, Seaside,
    831-883-3800)
Oakland 94612 (2221 Martin Luther King Jr. Way, 510-267-7820)
Oakland MHC 94607 (Oakland Army Base, 2505 West 14th St.,
    510-587-3434)
Oxnard 93030 (250 W. Citrus Grove Ave., Suite 150, 805-983-6384)
Palm Desert 92211 (41865 Boardwalk, Suite 103, 760-341-5570)
Pasadena 91776 (420 W. Las Tunas, San Gabriel, 626-289-5973)
Redding 96002 (351 Hartnell Ave., 530-226-7555)
Sacramento MHC 95655 (10633 Grissom Rd., 916-366-5420 or
    1-800-382-8387)
San Bruno 94066 (1011 Sneath Ln., Suite 300, 650-553-8000)
San Francisco 94107 (401 3rd St., 415-551-7300)
San Jose 95119 (80 Great Oaks Blvd., 408-363-3000)
San Luis Obispo 93401 (1288 Morro St., 200, 805-543-1233)
Santa Ana 92704 (2740 S. Bristol St., Ste. 110, 714-825-3500)
Santa Barbara 93110 (4440 Calle Real, 805-683-1491)
Santa Rosa 95404 (3315 Chanate Rd., 707-570-3855)
*Sepulveda 91343 (16111 Plummer St., 818-891-7711)
Sonora 95370 (19747 Greenley Rd., 209-588-2600)
South Los Angeles/Lynwood 90262 (3737 E. Martin Luther King Jr.,
Blvd., Suite 515, Lynwood, 310-537-6825)
Stockton 95231 (co-located with San Joaquin General Hospital, 500
    W. Hospital Rd., 209-946-3400)
Sun City 92586 (28125 Bradley Rd., 130, 951-672-1931)
Tulare 93274 (1050 N. Cherry St., 559-684-8703)
Ukiah 95482 (630 Kings Ct., 707-468-7700)
Upland 91786 (1238 E. Arrow Hwy. #100, 909-946-5348)

Victorville 92392 (12138 Industrial Blvd., Suite 120, 760-951-2599 or 1-800-741-8387)
Vista 92083 (1840 West Dr., 760-643-2000)
Whittier/Santa Fe Springs 90670 (10210 Orr and Day Rd., Santa Fe Springs, 562-864-5565)

**Regional Offices:**
Los Angeles 90024 (Fed. Bldg., 11000 Wilshire Blvd., serving counties of Inyo, Kern, Los Angeles, San Bernardino, San Luis Obispo, Santa Barbara and Ventura, statewide 1-800-827-1000)
Oakland 94612 (1301 Clay St., Rm. 1300 North, serving all CA counties not served by the Los Angeles, San Diego, or Reno VA Regional Offices, 1-800-827-1000)
San Diego 92108 (8810 Rio San Diego Dr., serving Imperial, Orange, Riverside and San Diego, statewide 1-800-827-1000). The counties of Alpine, Lassen, Modoc, and Mono are served by the Reno, NV, Regional Office.

**Benefits Office:**
Sacramento 95827 (10365 Old Placerville Rd., 916-364-6500)

**Vet Centers:**
Anaheim 92805 (859 S. Harbor Blvd., 714-776-0161)
Chico 95926 (280 Cohasset Rd., Suite 100, 530-899-8549)
Concord 94520 (1899 Clayton Rd., Suite 140, 925-680-4526)
Corona 92879 (800 Magnolia Ave., 110, 951-734-0525)
East Los Angeles 90022 (5400 E. Olympic Blvd., 140, 323-728-9966)
Eureka 95501 (2830 G St., Suite A, 707-444-8271)
Fresno 93726 (3636 N. 1st St., Suite 112, 559-487-5660)
Gardena 90247 (1045 W. Redondo Beach Blvd., 150, Gardena, 310-767-1221)
Marina 93933 (455 Reservation Rd., Suite E, 408-384-1660)
North Bay 94928 (6225 State Farm Dr., Suite 101, 707-586-3295)
Oakland 94612 (1504 Franklin St., 200, 510-763-3904)
Redwood City 94062 (2946 Broadway St., 650-299-0672)
Sacramento 95825 (1111 Howe Ave., Suite 390, 916-566-7430)
San Bernardino 92408 (155 West Hospitality Lane, Suite 140, 909-890-0797)
San Diego 92103 (2900 6th Ave., 619-294-2040)
San Francisco 94102 (505 Polk St., 415-441-5051)
San Jose 95112 (278 N. 2nd St., 408-993-0729)
Sepulveda 91343 (9737 Haskell Ave., 818-892-9227)
Ventura 93001 (790 E. Santa Clara, Suite 100, 805-585-1860)
Vista 92083 (1830 West Dr., Suite 103, 760-643-2070)
West Los Angeles 90230 (5730 Uplander Way, Suite 100, Culver

City, 310-641-0326)
***National Cemeteries:***
Fort Rosecrans NC 92106 (P.O. Box 6237, Point Loma, San Diego,
    619-553-2084)
Golden Gate NC 94066 (1300 Sneath Ln., San Bruno,
    650-589-7737)
Los Angeles NC 90049 (950 South Sepulveda Blvd., 310-268-4675)
Riverside NC 92518 (22495 Van Buren Blvd., 951-653-8417)
Sacramento Valley VA NC 95620 (5810 Midway Rd., Dixon,
    707-693-2460)
San Francisco NC 94129 (P.O. Box 29012, Presidio of San
    Francisco, 650-589-7737)
San Joaquin Valley NC 95322 (32053 West McCabe Rd., Gustine,
    209-854-1040)


# COLORADO
***Medical Centers:***
*Grand Junction 81501 (2121 North Ave., 970-242-0731 or
    866-206-6415)
VA Eastern Colorado Health Care System
  Denver 80220 (1055 Clermont St., 303-399-8020 or
    1-888-336-8262)
***Clinics:***
Alamosa, CO 81101 (622 Del Sol Dr., 719-587-6800 or toll free
    1-866-659-0930)
Aurora 80045 (13001 East 17th Place, Bldg. 500, 2nd Floor,
    303-724-0190)
Colorado Springs 80905 (25 N. Spruce St., 719-327-5660 or
    1-800-278-3883)
Durango 81301 (400 S. Camino del Rio, 970-247-2214)
Fort Collins 80524 (1100 Poudre River Dr., 970-224-1550)
Greeley 80631 (2020 16th St., 970-313-0027)
LaJunta 81050 (1100 Carson Ave., Suite 104, 719-383-5195 or
    877-329-2625)
Lakewood 80228 (155 Van Gordon St., Suite 395, 303-914-2680)
Lamar 81052 (201 Kendall Dr., 719-336-5972 or 866-240-2279)
Montrose 81401 (4 Hillcrest Plaza Way, 970-249-7791)
Pueblo 81008 (4112 Outlook Blvd., 719-553-1000 or
    1-800-369-6748)
***Regional Office:***
Denver 80225 (Mailing Address: PO Box 25126. Physical Address:

155 Van Gordon St., Lakewood, 80228, statewide 1-800-827-1000)
***Vet Centers:***
Boulder 80302 (2336 Canyon Blvd., Suite 130, 303-440-7306)
Colorado Springs 80903 (416 E. Colorado Ave., 719-471-9992)
Denver 80230 (7465 E. First Ave., Ste. B, 303-326-0645)
***National Cemeteries:***
Fort Logan NC 80235 (3698 S. Sheridan Blvd., Denver,
     303-761-0117)
Fort Lyon NC 81038 (303-761-0117)

# CONNECTICUT
***Medical Centers:***
Connecticut Health Care System:
     *West Haven Division 06516 (950 Campbell Ave., 203-932-5711)
     Newington Division 06111 (555 Willard Ave., 860-666-6951)
***Clinics:***
Danbury 06810 (7 Germantown Rd., 203-798-8422)
New London 06320 (15 Mohegan Ave., 860-437-3611)
Stamford 06905 (1275 Summer St., Suite 102, 203-325-0649)
Waterbury 06706 (133 Scovill St., Suite 203, 203-465-5292)
Windham 06226 (96 Mansfield St., 860-450-7583)
Winsted 06098 (115 Spencer St., 860-738-6985)
***Regional Office:***
Hartford (Bldg 2E – RM 5137, 555 Willard Ave.; Newington, 06111-
     2693, statewide 1-800-827-1000)
***Vet Centers:***
Norwich 06360 (2 Cliff St., 860-887-1755)
Wethersfield 06109 (30 Jordan Lane, 860-563-2320)
West Haven 06516 (141 Captain Thomas Blvd., 203-932-9899)

# DELAWARE
***Medical Center:***
*Wilmington 19805 (1601 Kirkwood Hwy., 302-994-2511 or
     1-800-461-8262)

***Clinics:***
Millsboro 19966 (214 W. DuPont Hwy., 302-934-0195)
Seaford 19973 (121 S. Front St., 302-628-8324)
***Regional Office:***
Wilmington 19805 (1601 Kirkwood Hwy., local, 302-994-2511)

*Vet Center:*
Wilmington 19805 (1601 Kirkwood Hwy., Bldg. 3, 302-994-1660)

## DISTRICT OF COLUMBIA
*Medical Center:*
*Washington, D.C. 20422 (50 Irving St., N.W., 202-745-8000)
*Clinic:*
Southeast 20032 (820 Chesapeake St., S.E., 202-745-8685)
*Regional Office:*
Washington, D.C., 20421 (1722 I St., N.W., local, 1-800-827-1000)
*Vet Center:*
Washington, D.C. 20011 (1250 Taylor St., N.W., 202-726-5212)

## FLORIDA
*Medical Centers:*
#*Bay Pines 33744 (10000 Bay Pines Blvd., 727-398-6661)
North Florida/South Georgia Veterans Health System:
    *Gainesville 32608 (1601 Southwest Archer Rd., 352-376-1611)
    *Lake City 32025 (619 S. Marion Ave., 386-755-3016)
*Miami 33125 (1201 N.W. 16th St., 305-575-7000)
*Tampa 33612 (13000 Bruce B. Downs Blvd., 813-972-2000)
*West Palm Beach 33410 (7305 N. Military Trail, 561-422-8262)
*Clinics:*
Boca Raton 33433 (900 Glades Rd., 561-416-8995)
Brevard 32940 (2900 Veterans Way, Viera, 321-637-3788)
Brooksville 34613 (14540 Cortez Blvd., 352-597-8287)
Coral Springs 33065 (9900 W. Sample Rd., Suite 100,
    954-575-4940)
Daytona Beach 32114 (551 National Health Care Dr., 386-323-7500)
Deerfield Beach 33442 (2100 SW 10th St., 954-570-5572)
Delray Beach 33445 (4800 Linton Blvd, 561-495-1973)
Dunedin 34698 (1721 Main St., 727-734-5276)
Ellenton 34222 (4333 U.S. Hwy 301 North, 941-721-0649)
Fort Myers 33916 (3033 Winkler Extension, 239-939-3939)
Ft. Pierce 34950 (727 North US 1, 772-595-5150)
Hollywood 33021 (3702 Washington St., Hollywood Pav., Suite 201,
    954-986-1811)
Homestead 33030 (950 Krome Ave., Suite 401, 305-248-0874)
Jacksonville 32206 (1833 Boulevard St., 904-232-2751)
Key Largo 33037 (105662 Overseas Hwy., 305-451-0164)
Key West 33040 (1300 Douglas Cir., 305-293-4609)

Kissimmee 34741 (201 Hilda St., Kissimmee, 407-518-5004)
Lakeland 33803 (3240 S. Florida Ave., Lakeland, 863-701-2470)
Lecanto 34461 (2804 Marc Knighton Ct., Suite A, 352-746-8000)
Leesburg 34748 (711 West Main St., 352-435-4000)
Miami OSAC 33135 (1492 West Flagler St., Suite 102,
    305-541-8435)
Naples 34101 (2685 Horseshoe Dr., Suite 101, 239-659-9188)
New Port Richey 34654 (9912 Little Rd., 727-869-4100)
Oakland Park 33334 (5599 N. Dixie Hwy., 954-771-2101)
Ocala 34470 (1515 E. Silver Springs Blvd., 352-369-3320)
Okeechobee 34972 (1201 N. Parrott Ave., 863-824-3232)
#*Orlando 32803 (5201 Raymond St., 407-629-1599)
Panama City 32407 (6703 West Hwy. 98, Bldg. 387, 850-636-7000)
Pembroke Pines 33024 (7369 Sheridan St., Suite 102,
    954-894-1668)
Pensacola South 32503 (312 Kenmore Rd., 850-476-1100)
Pensacola North 32506 (7895-C Pensacola Blvd., 850-476-1100)
Port Charlotte 33952 (4161 Tamiami Trail, 941-235-2710)
Sanford 32771 (1403 Medical Plaza Dr., 109, 407-323-5999)
Sarasota 34233 (5682 Bee Ridge Rd., Suite 100, 941-371-3349)
Sebring 33870 (3760 US Hwy. 27 South, 863-471-6227)
St. Augustine 32086 (1955 US 1 South, Suite 200, 904-829-0814)
St. Petersburg 33711 (3420 8th Ave., South, 727-322-1304)
Stuart 34997 (3501 SE Willoughby Blvd., 772-288-0304)
Tallahassee 32308 (1607 St. James Ct., 850-878-0191)
The Villages 32162 (1950 Laurel Manor Dr., Bldg. 204,
    352-205-8900)
Vero Beach 32960 (372 17th St., 772-299-4623)
Zephyrhills 33531 (6937 Medical View Ln., 813-780-2550)
### Regional Office:
St. Petersburg 33708 (mailing address: P.O. Box 1437; physical
    address: 9500 Bay Pines Blvd., statewide 1-800-827-1000)
### Benefits Offices:
Fort Lauderdale 33301 (VR&E, 299 East Broward Blvd., Room 324,
    1-800-827-1000)
Jacksonville 32256 (VR&E, 7825 Baymeadows Way, Suite 120-B,
    1-800-827-1000)
Orlando 32801 (1000 Legion Pl., VRE-Suite 1500, C&P-Suite 1550,
    1-800-827-1000)
Pensacola 32503-7492 (C&P, 312 Kenmore Rd., Rm. 1G250,
    1-800-827-1000)
West Palm Beach 33410 (C&P, 7305 North Military Tr., Suite 1A-167,

1-800-827-1000)

### *Vet Centers:*
Fort Lauderdale 33304 (713 N.E. 3rd Ave., 954-356-7926)
Jacksonville 32202 (300 East State St., 904-232-3621)
Miami 33122 (8280 NW 27th St., Suite 511, 305-859-8387)
Orlando 32822 (5575 S. Semoran Blvd., Suite 36, 407-857-2800)
Palm Beach 33461 (2311 10th Ave., North 13, 561-585-0441)
Pensacola 32501 (4501 Twin Oaks Dr., 850-456-5886)
Sarasota 34231 (4801 Swift Rd., 941-927-8285)
Saint Petersburg 33713 (2880 1st Ave., N., 727-893-3791)
Tallahassee 32303 (548 Bradford Rd., 850-942-8810)
Tampa 33604 (8900 N. Armenia Ave., Ste. 312, 813-228-2621)

### *National Cemeteries:*
Barrancas NC 32508-1099 (80 Hovey Rd., Naval Air Station,
    Pensacola, 850-453-4846)
Bay Pines NC 33504-0477 (10000 Bay Pines Blvd., North Bay Pines,
    727-398-9426)
Florida NC 33513 (6502 SW 102nd Ave., Bushnell, 352-793-7740)
Saint Augustine NC 32084 (104 Marine St., 352-793-7740)
South Florida NC 33467 (6501 South State Road 7, 561-649-6489)

## GEORGIA
### *Medical Centers:*
*Augusta 30904 (1 Freedom Way, 706-733-0188)
*Decatur 30033 (1670 Clairmont Rd., 404-321-6111)
#*Dublin 31021 (1826 Veterans Blvd., 478-272-1210)

### *Clinics:*
Albany 31701 (417 4th Ave., 229-446-9000 or 1-877-216-4495)
Athens 30610 (9249 Hwy 29 North, 706-227-4534)
Columbus 31906 (1310 13th Ave., 706-257-7200)
East Point 30344 (1513 Cleveland Ave., 404-321-6111)
Lawrenceville 30043 (1970 Riverside Pkwy., 404-417-1750)
Macon 31220 (5398 Thomaston Rd., Suite B, 478-476-8868 or
    1-800-552-7483)
Oakwood 30566 (3931 Mundy Mill Rd., Suite C, 404-728-8210)
Savannah 31406 (325 W. Montgomery Crossroad, 912-920-0214)
Smyrna 30082 (582 Concord Rd., 404-417-1760)
Valdosta 31602 (2841 North Patterson, 229-293-0132)
### *Regional Office:*
Decatur 30033 (1700 Clairmont Rd., statewide 1-800-827-1000)

***Vet Centers:***
Atlanta 30324 (1440 Dutch Valley Place, Suite G, 404-347-7264)
Savannah 31406 (8110A White Bluff Rd., 912-652-4097)
***National Cemeteries:***
Georgia NC 30114 (2025 Mt. Carmel Church Lane, Canton,
    866-236-8159)
Marietta NC 30060 (500 Washington Ave., 866-236-8159)


# GUAM
***Clinic:***
Agana Heights 96919 (U.S. Naval Hospital, Bldg-1, E-200, Box
    7608, 671-344-9200)
***Benefits Office/Vet Center:***
Hagatna 96910 (222 Chalan Santo Papa St., Ste. 202,
    671-472-7217)


# HAWAII
***Medical Center:***
Honolulu 96819-1522 (Pacific Islands Health Sys., 459 Patterson
    Rd., 808-433-0600)
***Clinics:***
Hilo 96720 (1285 Wainuenue Ave., Suite 211, 808-935-3781)
Honolulu PTSD 96819 (3375 Koapaka St., 808-566-1546)
Kauai; Lihue 96766 (3-3367 Kuhio Hwy., Suite 200, 808-246-0497)
Kona; Kailua-Kona 96740 (75-5995 Kuakini Hwy., Suite 413,
    808-329-0774)
Maui; Kahului 96732 (203 Ho'ohana St., Suite 303, 808-871-2454)
***Regional Office:***
Honolulu 96819-1522 (459 Patterson Rd., E Wing. Mailing address:
    PO Box 29020, Honolulu, HI 96820) (toll-free from Hawaii,
    Guam, Saipan, Rota and Tinian, 1-800-827-1000; toll-free
    from American Samoa, 1-877-899-4400)
***Benefits Offices:***
Hilo 96720 (VR&E, 891 Ululani St., 808-961-3413)
Kahului 96732 (VR&E, 203 Ho'ohana St., 808-873-9426)
***Vet Centers:***
Hilo 96720 (120 Keawe St., Suite 201, 808-969-3833)
Honolulu 96814 (1680 Kapiolani Blvd., Suite F.3, 808-973-8387)
Kailua-Kona 96740 (Pottery Terrace, Fern Bldg., 75-5995 Kuakini
    Hwy., # 415, 808-329-0574)
Lihue 96766 (3-3367 Kuhio Hwy., Suite 101, 808-246-1163)

Wailuku 96793 (35 Lunalilo, Suite 101, 808-242-8557)
***National Cemetery:***
National Cemetery of the Pacific 96813-1729 (2177 Puowaina Dr.,
     Honolulu, 808-532-3720)

## IDAHO
***Medical Center:***
*Boise 83702 (500 West Fort St., 208-422-1000)
***Clinics:***
Pocatello 83201 (444 Hospital Way, Suite 801, 208-232-6214)
Twin Falls 83301 (260 2nd Ave, E., 208-732-0947)
***Regional Office:***
Boise 83702 (805 W. Franklin St., statewide, 1-800-827-1000)
***Vet Centers:***
Boise 83705 (5440 Franklin Rd., Suite 100, 208-342-3612)
Pocatello 83201 (1800 Garrett Way, 208-232-0316)

## ILLINOIS
***Medical Centers:***
Chicago 60612 (Jesse Brown VA, 820 S. Damen Ave.,
     312-569-8387)
* VA Illiana Health Care System 61832 (Danville Med. Ctr., 1900 E.
     Main St., 217-554-3000 or 1-800-320-8387)
*Hines 60141 (Roosevelt Rd. & 5th Ave., 708-202-8387)
*Marion 62959 (2401 W. Main St., 618-997-5311)
#*North Chicago 60064 (3001 Green Bay Rd., 847-688-1900)
***Clinics:***
Aurora 60506 (1700 N. Landmark Rd., 630-859-2504)
Belleville 62223 (6500 W. Main St., 618-398-2100)
Chicago--Lakeside 60611 (333 E. Huron, 312-569-8387)
Chicago 60643 (2038 W. 95th St., 773-239-7134)
Chicago Heights 60411 (30 E. 15th St., Suite 207, 708-756-5454)
Decatur 62526 (3035 E. Mound Rd., 217-875-2670)
Effingham 62401 (Lincolnland Bldg., 1901 S. 4th St., 217-347-7600)
Elgin 60120 (450 Dundee Ave., Suite 100, 847-742-5920)
Evanston 60202 (107 -109 Clyde St., 847-869-6315)
Freeport 61032 (1301 Kiwanis Dr., 608-280-7038)
Galesburg 61401 (387 E. Grove St., 309-343-0311)
Joliet 60435 (2000 Glenwood Ave., 815-744-0492)
LaSalle 61301 (2970 Chartres St., 815-223-9678)
Manteno 60950 (One Veterans Dr., 815-468-1027)

McHenry 60050 (620 S. Route 31, 815-759-2306)
Mt. Vernon 62864 (1 Doctors Park Rd., 618-246-2910 or 2911)
Oak Lawn 60453 (4700 W. 95th St., Suite 104, 708-499-3675)
Oak Park 60302 (149 S. Oak Park Ave., 708-386-3008)
Peoria 61605 (411 Martin Luther King Jr. Dr., 309-497-0790)
Quincy 62301 (1707 North 12th St., 217-224-3366)
Rockford 61108 (4940 East State St., 815-227-0081)
Springfield 62702 (700 N. 7th St., Suite C, 217-522-9730)
***Regional Office:***
Chicago 60612 (2122 W. Taylor St., statewide 1-800-827-1000)
***Vet Centers:***
Chicago 60643 (2038 W. 95th St., Suite 200, 773-881-9900)
Chicago Heights 60411 (1600 S. Halsted St., 708-754-0340)
East St. Louis 62203 (1265 N. 89th St., Suite 5, 618-397-6602)
Evanston 60202 (565 Howard St., 847-332-1019)
Moline 61265 (1529 46th Ave., 6, 309-762-6954)
Oak Park 60302 (155 S. Oak Park Blvd., 708-383-3225)
Peoria 61603 (3310 N. Prospect Rd., 309-671-7300)
Springfield 62702 (624 S. 4th St., 217-492-4955)
***National Cemeteries:***
Abraham Lincoln NC 60421 (27034 South Diagonal Rd., Elwood,
    815-423-9958)
Alton NC 62003 (600 Pearl St., 314-260-8720)
Camp Butler NC 62707 (5063 Camp Butler Rd., Springfield,
    217-492-4070)
Danville NC 61832 (1900 East Main St., 217-554-4550)
Mound City NC 62963 (Junction Hwy., 37 & 51, 314-260-8720)
Quincy NC 62301 (36th and Maine St., 309-782-2094)
Rock Island NC 61299-7090 (Rock Island Arsenal, Bldg. 118,
    309-782-2094)


# INDIANA
***Medical Centers:***
Indianapolis 46202 (1481 W. 10th St., 317-554-0000)
Northern Indiana Health Care System:
    *Fort Wayne 46805 (2121 Lake Ave., 260-426-5431)
    *Marion 46953 (1700 E. 38th St., 765-674-3321)
***Clinics:***
Bloomington 47403 (455 S. Landmark Ave., 812-336-5723)
Crown Point 46307 (9330 S. Broadway, 219-662-5000)
Evansville 47713 (500 E. Walnut, 812-465-6202)

Greendale 47025 (1600 Flossie Dr., 812-539-2313)
Lawrenceburg 47025 (710 W. Eads Pkwy., 812-539-2313)
Muncie/Anderson 47304 (3500 W. Purdue Ave., 765-284-6822)
New Albany 47150 (811 Northgate Boulevard, 502-287-4100)
Richmond 47374 (4351 South A St., 765-973-6915)
South Bend 46614 (55725 S. Ironwood Rd., 574-229-4847 or tollfree
    1-866-436-1291)
Terre Haute 47802 (110 W. Honey Creek Pkwy., 812-232-2890)
West Lafayette 47906 (3851 N. River Rd., 765-464-2280 or
    1-800-320-8387)

**Regional Office:**
Indianapolis 46204 (575 N. Pennsylvania St., statewide
    1-800-827-1000)

**Vet Centers:**
Evansville 47711 (311 N. Weinbach Ave., 812-473-5993 or
    473-6084)
Fort Wayne 46802 (528 West Berry St., 260-460-1456)
Merrillville 46410 (6505 Broadway Ave., 219-736-5633)
Indianapolis 46208 (3833 N. Meridian St., Suite 120, 317-927-6440)

**National Cemeteries:**
Crown Hill NC 46208 (700 W. 38th St., Indianapolis, 765-674-0284)
Marion NC 46952 (1700 E. 38th St., 765-674-0284)
New Albany NC 47150 (1943 Ekin Ave., 502-893-3852)

# IOWA
**Medical Centers:**
Central Iowa Health Care System:
    #Des Moines 50310 (3600 30th St., 1-800-294-8387)
    #*Knoxville 50138 (1515 W. Pleasant St., 1-800-816-8878)
Iowa City 52246 (601 Hwy. 6 West, 319-338-0581)

**Clinics:**
Bettendorf 52722 (2979 Victoria St., 563-332-8528)
Dubuque 52001 (200 Mercy Dr., Suite 106, 563-589-8899)
Fort Dodge 50501 (804 Kenyon Rd., Suite 160, 515-576-2235)
Mason City 50401 (910 N. Eisenhower, 641-421-8077 or
    1-800-351-4671)
Sioux City 51104 (1551 Indian Hills Dr., Suite 206, 712-258-4700)
Waterloo 50701 (1015 S. Hackett Rd., 319-235-1235)

**Regional Office:**
Des Moines 50309 (210 Walnut St., Rm. 1063, statewide
    1-800-827-1000)

### Vet Centers:
Cedar Rapids 52402 (1642 42nd St. N.E., 319-378-0016)
Des Moines 50310 (2600 Martin Luther King Jr. Pkwy.,
    515-284-4929)
Sioux City 51104 (1551 Indian Hills Dr., Suite 204, 712-255-3808)
### National Cemetery:
Keokuk NC 52632 (1701 J St., 309-782-2094)


## KANSAS
### Medical Centers:
Eastern Kansas Health Care System:
    #*Leavenworth 66048 (4101 S. 4th St., Trafficway,
        913-682-2000)
    *Topeka 66622 (2200 SW Gage Blvd., 785-350-3111)
    *Wichita 67218 (5500 E. Kellogg, 316-685-2221)
### Clinics:
Abilene 67410 (510 NE 10th St., 785-263-2100, extension 161)
Chanute 66720 (629 S. Plummer, 620-431-4000, extension 1553)
Fort Dodge City 67801 (300 Custer, 620-225-7146)
Emporia 66801 (1201 W. 12th St., 620-343-6800, extension 1599)
Fort Scott 66701 (710 W. 8th St., 620-223-8400)
Garnett 66032 (421 S. Maple, 785-448-3131, extension 309)
Hays 67601 (207B E. 7th St., 785-625-3550)
Holton 66436 (1110 Columbine Dr., 785-364-2116, extension 115)
Junction City 66441 (715 Southwind Dr., 1-800-574-8387,
    extension 54670)
Kansas City 66102 (21 N. 12th St., Ste. 200, 1-800-952-8387
    extension 6990)
Lawrence 66044 (2200 Harvard St., 1-800-574-8387, or
    785-841-2957)
Liberal 67901 (2 Rock Island Rd., Suite 200, 620-626-5574)
Paola 66071 (501 S Hospital Dr., Suite 100, 816-922-2160)
Parsons 67357 (1401 N. Main St., 620-423-3858)
Russell 67665 (200 South Main St., 785-483-3131)
Salina 67401 (1410 East Iron, Suite 1, 785-826-1580)
Seneca 66538 (1600 Community Dr., 785-336-6181, extension 162)
### Regional Office:
Wichita 67218 (Robert J. Dole Regional Office, 5500 E. Kellogg Ave.,
    1-800-827-1000)
### Vet Center:
Wichita 67211 (413 S. Pattie, 316-265-3260)

### National Cemeteries:
Fort Leavenworth NC 66027 (913-758-4105)
Fort Scott NC 66701 (P.O. Box 917, 900 East Nat'l, 620-223-2840)
Leavenworth NC 66048 (P.O. Box 1694, 913-758-4105)

# KENTUCKY
### Medical Centers:
#* Fort Thomas 41075 (1000 S. Ft. Thomas Ave., 513-861-3100)
*Lexington 40502-2236 (1101 Veterans Dr., 859-233-4511)
Louisville 40206 (800 Zorn Ave., 502-287-4000)
### Clinics:
Bellevue 41073 (103 Landmark Dr., 859-392-3840)
Bowling Green 42103 (1110 Wilkinson Trace Cir., Harland Medical
     Plaza, 270-796-3590)
Florence 41042 (7711 Ewing, 859-282-4480)
Fort Campbell 42223 (Desert Storm Ave., Bldg. 61639,
     270-798-4118)
Fort Knox 40121 (851 Ireland Loop, 502-624-9396)
Hanson 42413 (926 Veterans Dr., 270-322-8019)
Louisville/Dupont 40207 (4010 Dupont Circle, 502-287-6986)
Louisville/Shively 40216 (3934 N. Dixie Hwy., Suite 210,
     502-287-6000)
Louisville/Standiford Field 40213 (1101 Grade Lane, 502-364-9635)
Paducah 42001 (1800 Clark St., 270-444-8465)
Prestonsburg 41653 (5230 KY Rt. 321, Suite 8, 606-886-1970)
Somerset 42501 (104 Hardin Lane, 606-676-0786)
### Regional Office:
Louisville 40202 (321 W. Main St., Ste., 390, statewide
     1-800-827-1000)
### Vet Centers:
Lexington 40507 (301 E. Vine St., Suite C, 859-253-0717)
Louisville 40208 (1347 S. 3rd St., 502-634-1916)
### National Cemeteries:
Camp Nelson NC 40356 (6980 Danville Rd., Nicholasville,
     859-885-5727)
Cave Hill NC 40204 (701 Baxter Ave., Louisville, 502-893-3852)
Danville NC 40442 (277 N. First St., 859-885-5727)
Lebanon NC 40033 (20 Highway 208, 502-893-3852)
Lexington NC 40508 (833 W. Main St., 859-885-5727)
Mill Springs NC 42544 (9044 West Highway 80, Nancy,
     859-885-5727)

Zachary Taylor NC 40207 (4701 Brownsboro Rd., Louisville,
    502-893-3852)


# LOUISIANA
*Medical Centers:*
*Alexandria 71306 (2495 Shreveport Hwy., 318-473-0010)
*New Orleans 70112 (1601 Perido St., 504-568-0811 ext. 2929
    or 1-800-935-8387)
Shreveport 71101 (510 E. Stoner Ave., 318-221-8411)
*Clinics:*
Baton Rouge 70809 (7968 Essen Park Ave., 225-761-6700)
Hammond VA Mobile Clinic 70403 (1131 S. Morrison Ave.,
    985-340-7816)
Jennings 70546 (1907 Johnson St., 337-824-1000)
Lafayette 70501 (2100 Jefferson St. 337-261-0734)
LaPlace 70068 (501 Rue de Sante, Suite 10, 1-800-935-8387)
Monroe 71203 (250 DeSiard Plaza, 318-343-6100)
Slidell 70461 (340 Gateway Dr., 1-800-935-8387)
*Regional Office:*
Gretna 70054 (mailing address: PO Box 1278; physical address:
    671A Whitney Ave., Gretna, GA  70056, statewide
    1-800-827-1000)
*Vet Centers:*
Kenner 70062 (2200 Veterans Blvd., Suite 114, 504-464-4743)
Shreveport 71104 (2800 Youree Dr., Bldg. 1, Suite 1, 318-861-1776)
*National Cemeteries:*
Alexandria NC 71360 (209 E. Shamrock St., Pineville,
    601-445-4981)
Baton Rouge NC 70806 (220 N. 19th St., 225-654-3767)
Port Hudson NC 70791 (20978 Port Hickey Rd., Zachary,
    225-654-3767)


# MAINE
*Medical Center:*
*Augusta 04330 (1 VA Center, 207-623-8411)
*Regional Office:*
Togus 04330 (1 VA Center, Building 248, Room 205, 877-421-8263)
*Clinics:*
Bangor 04401 (304 Hancock St., Suite 3B, 207-561-3600)
Calais 04619 (50 Union St., 207-904-3700)
Caribou 04736 (163 Van Buren Dr., Suite 6, 207-493-3800)

Rumford 04276 (431 Franklin St., 207-369-3200)
Saco 04072 (655 Main St., 207-294-3100)
***Vet Centers:***
Bangor 04401 (352 Harlow St., 207-947-3391)
Caribou 04736 (456 York St., Irving Complex, 207-496-3900)
Lewiston 04240 (Pkwy Complex, 29 Westminster St., 207-783-0068)
Portland 04103 (475 Stevens Ave., 207-780-3584)
Springvale 04083 (628 Main St., 207-490-1513)
***National Cemetery:***
Togus NC 04330 (1 VA Center; 508-563-7113)


# MARYLAND
***Medical Centers:***
Maryland Health Care System:
    *Baltimore 21201 (10 N. Green St., 410-605-7000)
    #Perry Point 21902 (Bldg. 5H, 410-642-2411)
Baltimore 21218 (Rehab. & Extended Care, 3900 Loch Raven Blvd.,
    410-605-7000)
***Clinics:***
Cambridge 21613 (830 Chesapeake Dr., 410-228-6243)
Charlotte Hall 20622 (29431 Charlotte Hall Rd., 301-884-7102)
Cumberland 21502 (200 Glenn St., 301-724-0061)
Fort Howard 21052 (9600 North Point Rd., 410-477-1800)
Glen Burnie 21061 (1406 South Crain Hwy., 410-590-4140)
Greenbelt 20770 (7525 Greenway Center Dr., Suite T-4,
    301-345-2463)
Hagerstown 21742 (1101 Opal Court, 301-665-1462)
Loch Raven 21218 (3901 The Alameda, 410-605-7650)
Pocomoke 21851 (101 Market St., 410-957-6718)
***Regional Office:***
Baltimore 21201 (31 Hopkins Plaza Federal Bldg., 1-800-827-1000)
***Vet Centers:***
Baltimore 21207 (6666 Security Blvd., Suite 2, 410-277-3600)
Cambridge 21613 (5510 West Shore Dr., 410-228-6305 ext. 4123)
Elkton 21921 (103 Chesapeake Blvd. Suite A, 410-392-4485)
Silver Spring 20910 (1015 Spring St., Suite 101, 301-589-1073)
***National Cemeteries:***
Annapolis NC 21401 (800 West St., 410-644-9696)
Baltimore NC 21228 (5501 Frederick Ave., 410-644-9696)
Loudon Park NC 21228 (3445 Frederick Ave., Baltimore,
    410-644-9696)

## MASSACHUSETTS
### Medical Centers:
Bedford 01730 (200 Springs Rd., 1-800-838-6331 or 781-275-7500)
Boston 02130 (150 S. Huntington Ave., 617-232-9500)
Brockton 02301 (940 Belmont St., 508-583-4500)
*Northampton 01053-9764 (421 N. Main St., 413-584-4040)
West Roxbury 02132 (1400 VFW Pkwy., 617-323-7700)
### Clinics:
Boston 02114 (251 Causeway St., 617-248-1000)
Dorchester 02124 (895 Blue Hill Ave., 617-822-7146)
Edgartown 02539 (55 Simpson's Lane, 508-627-1044)
Fitchburg 01420 (275 Nichols Rd., 978-342-9781)
Framingham 01702 (61 Lincoln St., 508-628-0205)
Franklin County 01301 (51 Sanderson St., Ste. 9, 413-773-8428)
Gloucester 01930 (298 Washington St., 978-282-0676)
Haverhill 01830 (108 Merrimack St., 978-372-5207)
Hyannis 02601 (145 Falmouth Rd., 508-771-3190)
Lowell 01852 (130 Marshall Rd., 978-671-9000)
Lynn 01904 (225 Boston St., Suite 107, 781-595-9818)
Martha's Vineyard Hospital 02557 (Linton Lane, Oak Bluffs,
     508-693-0410)
Nantucket Cottage Hospital 02554 (57 Prospect St., 508-228-1200)
New Bedford 02740 (175 Elm St., 508-994-0217)
Pittsfield 01201 (73 Eagle St., 413-443-4857)
Quincy 02169 (114 Whitwell St., 2nd Floor, 617-376-2010)
Springfield 01104 (25 Bond St., 413-731-6000)
Worcester 01605 (605 Lincoln St., 508-856-0104)
### Regional Office:
Boston 02203-0393 (JFK Federal Building, Government Center,
     Room 1425, statewide 1-800-827-1000)  (Towns of Fall River &
     New Bedford, counties of Barnstable, Dukes, Nantucket, Bristol,
     part of Plymouth served by Providence, R.I., VA Regional Office)
### Vet Centers:
Boston 02215 (665 Beacon St., 617-424-0665)
Brockton 02401 (1041-L Pearl St., 508-580-2730)
Lowell 01852 (73 East Merrimack St., 978-453-1151)
New Bedford 02740 (468 North St., 508-999-6920)
Springfield 01103 (1985 Main St., Northgate Plaza, 413-737-5167)
Worcester 01605 (597 Lincoln St., 508-856-7428)
### National Cemetery:
Massachusetts NC 02532 (Connery Ave., Bourne, 508-563-7113)

# MICHIGAN
*Medical Centers:*
*Ann Arbor 48105 (2215 Fuller Rd., 734-769-7100)
*Battle Creek 49015 (5500 Armstrong Rd., 269-966-5600)
*Detroit 48201 (4646 John R. St., 313-576-1000)
*Iron Mountain 49801 (325 East H St., 906-774-3300 or
     1-800-215-8262 in Michigan & Wisconsin)
*Saginaw 48602 (1500 Weiss St., 989-497-2500)
*Clinics:*
Benton Harbor 49022 (115 Main St., 269-934-9123)
Flint 48532 (G-3267 Beecher Rd., 810-720-2913)
Gaylord 49735 (806 S. Otsego, 989-732-6555)
Grand Rapids 49505 (3019 Coit, N.E., 616-365-9575)
Hancock 49930-1495 (890 Campus Dr., 906-482-7762)
Ironwood 49938 (930 Cloverland Dr., 906-932-0032)
Jackson 49203 (400 Hinckley Blvd., Suite 300, 517-782-7415)
Kincheloe 49788 (16523 S. Watertower Dr., 1, 906-495-3030)
Lansing 48824 (2025 S. Washington Ave., 517-267-3925)
Marquette 49855 (425 Fisher St., 906-226-4618)
Menominee 49858 (1101 11th Ave., Suite 2, 906-863-1286)
Muskegon 49442 (165 E. Apple Ave., Suite 201, 231-725-4105)
Oscoda 48750 (5671 Skeel Ave., Suite 4, 989-747-0026)
Pontiac 48340 (1701 Baldwin Ave., Suite 101, 248-409-0585)
Sault Ste. Marie 49788 (16523 S. Watertower Dr., 906-495-3030)
Traverse City 49684 (3271 Racquet Club Dr., 231-932-9720)
Yale 48097 (7470 Broadway Dr., 810-387-3211)
*Regional Office:*
Detroit 48226 (Patrick V. McNamara Federal Bldg., 477 Michigan
     Ave., Rm. 1400, 1-800-827-1000)
*Vet Centers:*
Dearborn 48124-3438 (2881 Monroe St., Suite 100, 313-277-1428)
Detroit 48201 (4161 Cass Ave., 313-831-6509)
Grand Rapids 49507 (1940 Eastern SE, 616-243-0385)
*National Cemeteries:*
Fort Custer NC 49012 (15501 Dickman Rd., Augusta, 269-731-4164)
Great Lakes NC 48442 (4200 Belford Rd., Holly, 866-348-8603)


# MINNESOTA
*Medical Centers:*
*Minneapolis 55417 (One Veterans Dr., 612-725-2000)
#*St. Cloud 56303 (4801 Veterans Dr., 320-252-1670)

## Clinics:
Brainerd 56401 (1777 Hwy. 18 East, 218-855-1115)
Fergus Falls 56537 (1821 North Park St., 218-739-1400)
Hibbing 55746 (1101 E. 37th St., Suite 220, 218-263-9698)
Mankato Area, 15 sites (612-725-1991)
Maplewood 55109 (2785 White Bear Ave., Suite 210, 651-290-3040)
Montevideo 56265 (1025 N. 13th St., 320-269-2222)
Rochester 55902 (1617 Skyline Dr., 507-252-0885)
Saint James 56081 (1205 6th Ave. South, 507-375-3391)

## Regional Office:
St. Paul 55111 (Bishop Henry Whipple Federal Bldg., 1 Federal Dr.,
    1-800-827-1000) (Counties of Becker, Beltrami, Clay, Clearwa
    ter, Kittson, Lake of the Woods, Mahnomen, Marshall, Norman,
    Otter Tail, Pennington, Polk, Red Lake, Roseau, Wilkin served by
    Fargo, N.D., VA Regional Office)

## Vet Centers:
Duluth 55802 (405 E. Superior St., 218-722-8654)
St. Paul 55114 (2480 University Ave., 651-644-4022)

## National Cemetery:
Fort Snelling NC 55450-1199 (7601 34th Ave. So., Minneapolis,
    612-726-1127)


# MISSISSIPPI

## Medical Centers:
#*Biloxi 39531 (400 Veterans Ave., 228-523-5000)
*Jackson 39216 (1500 E. Woodrow Wilson Dr., 601-364-7900)

## Clinics:
Byhalia 38611 (12 East Brunswick St., 662-838-2163)
Columbus 39702 (824 Alabama St., 662-244-0391)
Greenville 38703 (1502 S. Colorado St., 662-332-9872)
Hattiesburg 39401 (231 Methodist Blvd., 601-296-3530)
Kosciusko 39090 (332 Hwy. 12 W., 662-289-8089)
Meridian 39301 (2103 13th St., 601-482-3275)
Natchez 39120 (46 Sgt. Prentiss Dr., Suite 16, 601-442-7141)
Smithville 38870 3 sites (63420 Highway 25 North, for information
    call 901-523-8990)

## Regional Office:
Jackson 39216 (1600 E. Woodrow Wilson Ave., statewide
    1-800-827-1000)

## Vet Centers:
Biloxi 39531 (288 Veterans Ave., 228-388-9938)

Jackson 39216 (1755 Lelia Dr., Suite 104, 601-965-5727)
***National Cemeteries:***
Biloxi NC 39535-4968 (P.O. Box 4968, 400 Veterans Ave.,
    228-388-6668)
Corinth NC 38834 (1551 Horton St., 901-386-8311)
Natchez NC 39120 (41 Cemetery Rd., 601-445-4981)

# MISSOURI
***Medical Centers:***
*Columbia 65201 (800 Hospital Dr., 573-814-6000)
Kansas City 64128 (4801 Linwood Blvd., 816-861-4700)
*Poplar Bluff 63901 (1500 N. Westwood Blvd., 573-686-4151)
Saint Louis 63106 (915 N. Grand Blvd., 314-652-4100)
*Saint Louis 63125 (1 Jefferson Barracks Dr., 314-652-4100)
***Clinics:***
Belton 64012 (17140 Bel-Ray Place, 816-922-2161 or
    816-318-0251)
Camdenton 65020 (246 East Hwy. 54, 573-317-1150)
Cameron 64429 (1111 Euclid, 816-632-1369)
Cape Girardeau 63701 (2420 Veterans Memorial Dr., 573-339-0909)
Farmington 63640 (1580 W. Columbia Dr., 573-760-1365)
Fort Leonard Wood 65473 (126 Missouri Ave., 573-329-8305)
Kirksville 63501 (1108 East Patterson, Suite 9, 660-627-8387)
Mexico 65265 (One Veterans Dr., 573-581-9630)
Mount Vernon 65712 (600 N. Main St., 417-466-0118 or
    1-800-253-8387)
Nevada 64772 (322 Prewitt, 417-448-8905)
Salem 65560 (Hwy. 72 North, 573-729-6626, ext. 5230)
Saint Charles 63304 (7 Jason Court, 636-498-1113)
Saint James 65559 (620 N. Jefferson, 573-265-0448)
Saint Joseph 64506 (1314 N. 36th, 1-800-952-8387, ext. 6925)
Saint Louis 63136 (10600 Lewis and Clark Blvd., 314-286-6988)
Warrensburg 64093 (1300 Veterans Rd., 816-922-2500)
West Plains 65775 (1211 Missouri Ave., 417-257-2454)
***Regional Office:***
Saint Louis 63103 (400 South 18th St., statewide 1-800-827-1000)
***Benefits Office:***
Kansas City 64128 (4801 Linwood Blvd., 816-922-2660 or 1-800-
525-1483, x 52660)
***Vet Centers:***
Kansas City 64111 (301 E. Armour Rd., 816-753-1866)

Saint Louis 63103 (2345 Pine St., 314-231-1260)
**National Cemeteries:**
Jefferson Barracks NC 63125 (2900 Sheridan Rd., St. Louis,
    314-260-8720)
Jefferson City NC 65101 (1024 E. McCarty St., 314-260-8720)
Springfield NC 65804 (1702 E. Seminole St., 417-881-9499)


# MONTANA
**Medical Centers:**
Montana Health Care System
    Fort Harrison 59636 (1892 William St., 406-442-6410)
    *Miles City 59301 (210 S. Winchester, 406-874-5600)
**Clinics:**
Anaconda 59711 (118 E. 7th St., 406-563-6090)
Billings 59102 (2345 King Ave. W., 406-651-5670)
Bozeman 59715 (300 N. Wilson, Suite 703G, 406-522-8923)
Glasgow 59230 (621 3rd St. South, 406-228-3554)
Great Falls 59405 (1417-9th St. South, Suite 200, 1-877-468-8387)
Kalispell 59901 (66 Claremont St., Lower Level Suite B,
    406-751-5980)
Miles City 59301 (210 S. Winchester, 406-232-3060
Missoula 59808 (2687 Palmer St., Suite C, 1-877-468-8387)
Sidney 59270 (216 14th Avenue SW, 406-488-2307)
**Regional Office:**
Fort Harrison 59636 (1892 William St., Hwy., 12 West, statewide
    1-800-827-1000)
**Vet Centers:**
Billings 59102 (1234 Ave., C, 406-657-6071)
Missoula 59802 (500 N. Higgins Ave., 406-721-4918)


# NEBRASKA
**Medical Centers:**
VA Nebraska-Western Iowa Health Care System:
    *Grand Island 68803 (2201 N. Broadwell Ave., 308-382-3660 or
    1-800-451-5796)
    Omaha 68105 (4101 Woolworth Ave, 402-346-8800)
**Clinics:**
Alliance 69301 (524 Box Butte Ave., 1-800-764-5370)
Gering (Scottsbluff) 69341 (2540 N. 10th St., 308-220-3930)
Lincoln 68510 (600 S. 70th St., 402-489-3802)
Norfolk 68701 (301 N. 27th St., 402-844-8022)

North Platte 69101 (600 East Francis, Suite 3, 308-532-6906 or
1-800-451-8796)
Sidney 69162 (1116 10th Ave., 308-254-5575)
Scottsbluff 69341 (1441 E. 20th St., 308-220-3930 or
1-800-764-5370)
**Regional Office:**
Lincoln 68516 (5631 S. 48th St., statewide 1-800-827-1000)
**Vet Centers:**
Lincoln 68508 (920 L St., 402-476-9736)
Omaha 68131 (2428 Cuming St., 402-346-6735)
**National Cemetery:**
Fort McPherson NC 69151-1031 (12004 S. Spur 56A, Maxwell,
888-737-2800)

# NEVADA
**Medical Centers:**
Las Vegas Nellis Air Force Base 89191 (4700 N. Las Vegas Blvd.,
702-653-2227)
*Reno 89502 (1000 Locust St., 1-888-838-6256)

**Clinics:**
Carson Valley 89423 (925 Ironwood St., Suite 2102, 1-888-838-6256
extension 4000)
Ely 89301 (6 Steptoe Circle, 775-289-3612)
Henderson 89014 (2920 N. Green Valley Pkwy., Suite 215,
702-456-3825)
Las Vegas 89036 (PO Box 360001, N. Las Vegas, 702-636-3000)
Las Vegas 89102 (Psychiatric, 1501 S. Arville, 702-259-4646)
Las Vegas 89032 (2455 W. Cheyenne Ave., 702-636-6375)
Las Vegas 89109 (3131 La Canada St., 702-636-6360)
Las Vegas 89106 (901 Rancho Lane, 702-636-6370)
Las Vegas 89106 (Homeless Veterans, 405 N. Wilson,
702-386-3125)
Las Vegas 89118 (4420 W. Diablo Dr., 702-636-3000 ext. 4475)
Las Vegas 89106 (912 W. Owens Ave., 702-636-4077)
Las Vegas 89129 (2410 Fire Mesa St., 702-636-6320)
Las Vegas 89121 (4187 S Pecos Rd., 702-636-6350)
Las Vegas 89103 (3880 S. Jones Blvd., 702-636-6390)
Las Vegas 89030 (1841 E. Craig Rd., 702-636-3090)
Las Vegas 89106 (630 S. Rancho Rd., 702-636-6355)
Pahrump 89048 (2100 E. Calvada Blvd., 775-727-7535)

***Regional Office:***
Reno 89511 (5460 Reno Corporate Dr., statewide 1-800-827-1000)
***Benefits Office:***
Las Vegas 89107 (4800 Alpine Pl., Suite 12, 1-800-827-1000)
***Vet Centers:***
Las Vegas 89146 (1919 So. Jones Blvd., Suite A., 702-251-7873)
Reno 89503 (1155 W. 4th St., Suite 101, 775-323-1294)

## NEW HAMPSHIRE
***Medical Center:***
*Manchester 03104 (718 Smyth Rd., 603-624-4366 or
    1-800-892-8384)
***Clinics:***
Conway 03818 (7 Greenwood Ave., 603-447-2555)
Littleton 03561 (600 St. Johnsbury Rd., 603-444-9328)
Portsmouth 03803 (302 Newmarket St., 603-624-4366 ext. 5500, or
    1-800-892-8384)
Somersworth 03878 (200 Route 108, 603-4366, ext. 5700)
Tilton 03276 (139 Winter St., 603-624-4366 ext. 5600, or
    1-800-892-8384)
***Regional Office:***
Manchester 03101 (Norris Cotton Federal Bldg., 275 Chestnut St.,
    1-800-827-1000)
***Vet Center:***
Manchester 03104 (103 Liberty St., 603-668-7060/61)

## NEW JERSEY
***Medical Centers:***
New Jersey Health Care System:
    *East Orange 07018 (385 Tremont Ave., 973-676-1000)
    #*Lyons 07939 (151 Knollcroft Rd., 908-647-0180)
***Clinics:***
Brick 08724 (970 Rt. 70, 732-206-8900)
Cape May 08204 (U.S. Coast Guard Trng. Ctr., 1 Munro Ave.,
    609-898-8700)
Elizabeth 07206 (654 East Jersey St., 2nd Floor, 908-994-0120)
Fort Dix 08640 (Marshall Hall, 8th & Alabama, 609-562-2999)
Fort Monmouth 07703 (Patterson Army Health Clinic, Stephenson
        Ave., Bldg. 1075, 732-532-4500)
Hackensack 07601 (385 Prospect Ave., 201-487-1390)
Jersey City 07302 (115 Christopher Columbus Dr., 201-435-3055)

Morristown 07960 (340 West Hanover Ave., 973-539-9794)
Newark 07102 (20 Washington Pl., 973-645-1441)
New Brunswick 08901 (317 George St., 732-729-0646)
Paterson 07503 (275 Getty Ave., 973-247-1666)
Sewell 08080 (211 County House Rd., 856-401-7665)
Trenton 08611 (171 Jersey St., Bldg. 36, 609-989-2355)
Turnersville 08096 (160 Fries Mill Rd., 856-262-4140)
Ventnor 08406 (6601 Ventnor Ave., Suite 302, 609-823-3122)
Vineland 08360 (1051 W. Sherman Ave., 856-692-2881)

### Regional Office:
Newark 07102 (20 Washington Pl., statewide 1-800-827-1000)
(Philadelphia, PA Regional Office serves counties of Atlantic,
Burlington, Camden, Cape May, Cumberland, Gloucester,
Salem)

### Vet Centers:
Bloomfield 07003 (2 Broad St., Suite 703, 973-748-0980)
Jersey City 07302 (115 Christopher Columbus Dr., Suite 200,
973-645-2038)
Trenton 08611 (171 Jersey St., Bldg. 36, 609-989-2260)
Ventnor 08406 (6601 Ventnor Ave., Suite 105, 609-487-8387)

### National Cemeteries:
Beverly NC 08010 (916 Bridgeboro Rd., 609-877-5460)
Finn's Point NC 08079 (Box 542, R.F.D. 3, Fort Mott Rd., Salem,
609-877-5460)

# NEW MEXICO
### Medical Center:
*Albuquerque 87108 (1501 San Pedro Dr., SE., 505-265-1711 or
1-800-465-8262)

### Clinics:
Alamogordo 88310 (1410 Aspen, 505-437-9195)
Artesia 88210 (1700 W. Main St., 505-746-3531)
Clovis 88101 (921 E. Llano Estacada St., 505-763-4335)
Espanola 87532 (620 Coronado St., Suite-B, 505-753-7395)
Farmington 87401 (1001 W. Broadway, Suite C, 505-326-4383)
Gallup 87301 (320 State Hwy., 564, 505-722-7234)
Hobbs 88240 (1601 N. Turner, 505-391-0354)
Las Cruces 88011 (1635 Don Roser, 505-522-1241)
Las Vegas 87701 (1235 8th St., 505-425-6788)
Raton 87740 (1275 S. 2nd St., 505-445-2391)
Santa Fe 87507 (2213 Brothers Rd., Suite 600, 505-986-8645)

Silver City 88061 (1302 32nd St., 505-538-2921)
Truth or Consequences 87901 (1960 N. Date St., 505-894-7662)
**Regional Office:**
Albuquerque 87102 (Dennis Chavez Federal Bldg., 500 Gold Ave.,
    S.W., statewide 1-800-827-1000)
**Vet Centers:**
Albuquerque 87104 (1600 Mountain Rd. N.W., 505-346-6562)
Farmington 87402 (4251 E. Main, Suite C, 505-327-9684)
Santa Fe 87505 (2209 Brothers Rd., Suite 110, 505-988-6562)
**National Cemeteries:**
Fort Bayard NC 88036 (P.O. Box 189, 915-564-0201)
Santa Fe NC 87501 (501 N. Guadalupe St., 505-988-6400 or
    toll-free 877-353-6295)


# NEW YORK
**Medical Centers:**
*Albany 12208 (113 Holland Ave., 518-626-5000)
#*Canandaigua 14424 (400 Fort Hill Ave., 585-393-7100)
#*Bath 14810 (76 Veterans Ave., 607-664-4000)
*Bronx 10468 (130 W. Kingsbridge Rd., 718-584-9000)
VA New York Harbor Healthcare System:
    Brooklyn 11209 (800 Poly Place, 718-836-6600)
    New York 10010 (423 East 23rd St. (1st Ave.), 212-686-7500)
    #*St. Albans 11425 (179 Street & Linden Blvd., 718-526-1000)
VA Hudson Valley Healthcare System:
    *Castle Point 12511 (845-831-2000)
    #*Montrose 10548 (2094 Albany Post Rd., Route 9A/PO Box
    100, 914-737-4400)
*Northport 11768 (79 Middleville Rd., 631-261-4400)
*Syracuse 13210 (800 Irving Ave., 315-425-4400)
Western New York Health Care System:
    *Batavia 14020 (222 Richmond Ave., 585-297-1000)
    *Buffalo 14215 (3495 Bailey Ave., 716-834-9200)
**Clinics:**
Auburn 13201 (17 Lansing St., 315-255-7002)
Bainbridge 13733 (109 N. Main St., 607-967-8590)
Binghamton 13001 (425 Robinson St., 607-772-9100)
Brooklyn 11201 (40 Flatbush Ave. Ext., 8th Fl., 718-439-4300)
Bronx 10459 (953 Southern Blvd, 718-741-4900)
Buffalo 14209 (Homeless Veterans, 1298 Main St., 716-881-5855)
Buffalo 14214 (2963 Main St., 716-862-8865)

Carmel 10512 (1875 Route 6-Warwick Savings Bank, 2nd Floor,
    845-228-5291)
Carthage 13619 (3 Bridge St., 315-493-4180)
Catskill 12414 (159 Jefferson Heights, Columbia Greene Medical
    Arts Bldg., Suite A102, 518-943-7515)
Clifton Park 12065 (1673 Route 9, 518-383-8506)
Cortland 13405 (1129 Commons Ave., 607-662-1517)
Dunkirk 14048 (325 Central Ave., 716-366-2122)
Elizabethtown 12932 (Community Hospital, 75 Park St.,
    518-873-3295)
Elmira 14901 (200 Madison Ave. 877-845-3247, ext. 44640)
Fonda 12068 (2623 State Hwy., 30A, 518-853-1247)
Glens Falls 12801 (84 Broad St., 518-798-6066)
Goshen 10924 (30 Hatfield Ln., Suite 204, 845-294-6927)
Islip 11751 (39 Nassau Ave., 631-581-5330)
Ithaca 14850 (10 Arrowwood Dr., 607-274-4680)
Jamestown 14701 (890 East 2nd St., 716-661-1447)
Kingston 12401 (63 Hurley Ave., 845-331-8322)
Lackawanna 14218 (227 Ridge Rd., 716-822-5944)
Lindenhurst 11757 (560 N. Delaware Ave., 631-884-1133)
Lockport 14094 (5875 S. Transit Rd., 716-433-2025)
Malone 12953 (183 Park St., 518-481-2545)
Massena 13662 (1 Hospital Dr., 315-769-4253)
Monticello 12701 (461 Broadway, 845-791-4936)
New City 10956 (Citi Bank Building, Suite 400, 20 Squadron Blvd.
    845-634-8942)
New York 10027 (Harlem Care Center, 55 W. 125th St., 11th Floor,
    212-828-5265)
New York 10014 (Soho Center, 245 West Houston St.,
    212-337-2569)
New York 10011 (OSP Center, 437 W. 16th St., 212-462-4461)
Niagara Falls 14301 (2201 Pine Ave., 1-800-223-4810)
Olean 14760 (465 N. Union St., 716-373-7709)
Oswego 13126 (Seneca Hill Hlth. Cen., 105 County Rt. 45A, Suite
    400, 315-343-0925)
Patchogue 11772 (4 Phyllis Dr., 631-758-4419)
Pine Plains 12567 (2881 Church St., Rt. 199, 518-398-9240)
Plainview 11803 (1425 Old Country Rd., 516-694-6008)
Plattsburgh 12901 (43 Durkee St., Suite 300, 518-561-8310)
Port Jervis 12771 (150 Pike St. 845-856-5396)
Poughkeepsie 12603 (Freedom Exec. Park, 488 Freedom Plains
    Rd., Suite 120, 845-452-5151)

Riverhead 11901 (89 Hubbard Ave., 631-727-7171)
Rochester 14620 (465 Westfall Rd., 585-463-2600)
Rome 13441 (125 Brookley Rd., Building 510, 315-334-7100)
Schenectady 12308 (Sheridan Plaza, 1322 Gerling St.,
    518-346-3334)
Sidney 13733 (109 Main St., 607-967-8590)
Staten Island 10314 (1150 South Ave., 3rd Fl., Suite 301,
    718-761-2973)
Sunnyside, North Queens 11104 (41-03 Queens Blvd.,
    718-741-4800)
Troy 12180 (295 River St., 518-274-7707)
Warsaw 14569 (400 N. Main St., 585-786-2233)
Wellsville 14895 (13 Loder St., 585-596-2056)
Westhampton 11978 (150 Old Riverhead Rd., 631-898-0599)
White Plains 10601 (23 South Broadway, 914-421-1951)
Yonkers 10701 (124 New Main St., 914-375-8055)

**Regional Offices:**
Buffalo 14202 (Niagara Center, 130 S. Elmwood St., 1-800-827-
    1000) (Serves counties not served by New York City VA Regional
        Office.)
New York City 10014 (245 W. Houston St., statewide 1-800-827-
    1000) (Serves counties of Albany, Bronx, Clinton, Columbia,
    Delaware, Dutchess, Essex, Franklin, Fulton, Greene, Hamilton,
    Kings, Montgomery, Nassau, New York, Orange, Otsego,
    Putnam, Queens, Rensselaer, Richmond, Rockland,
    Saratoga, Schenectady, Schoharie, Suffolk, Sullivan,
    Ulster, Warren, Washington, Westchester.)

**Benefits Offices:**
Albany 12208 (113 Holland Ave., 1-800-827-1000)
Rochester 14620 (465 Westfall Rd., 1-800-827-1000)
Syracuse 13202 (344 W. Genesee St., 1-800-827-1000)

**Vet Centers:**
Albany 12206 (875 Central Ave., 518-438-2505)
Babylon 11702 (116 West Main St., 631-661-3930)
Bronx 10458 (130 West Kingsbridge Rd., Rm. 7A-13, 718-367-3500)
Brooklyn 11201 (25 Chapel St., Suite 604, 718-330-2825)
Buffalo 14202 (564 Franklin St., 716-882-0505)
New York 10004 (32 Broadway, Suite 200, 212-742-9591)
New York 10027 (55 West 125th St., 212-426-2200)
Rochester 14620 (1867 Mt. Hope Ave., 585-232-5040)
Staten Island 10301 (150 Richmond Terrace, 718-816-4499)
Syracuse 13210 (716 E. Washington St., 315-478-7127)

White Plains 10601 (300 Hamilton Ave., 914-682-6250)
Woodhaven 11421 (75-10B 91st Ave., 718-296-2871)
***National Cemeteries:***
Bath NC 14810 (76 Veterans Ave., San Juan Ave., 607-664-4853)
Calverton NC 11933-1031 (210 Princeton Blvd., 631-727-5410/5770)
Cypress Hills NC 11208 (625 Jamaica Ave., Brooklyn, 631-454-4949)
Long Island NC 11735-1211 (2040 Wellwood Ave., Farmingdale,
    631-454-4949)
Saratoga NC 12871-1721 (200 Duell Rd., Schuylerville,
    518-581-9128)
Woodlawn NC 14901 (1825 Davis St., Elmira, 607-732-5411)


# NORTH CAROLINA
***Medical Centers:***
*Asheville 28805 (1100 Tunnel Rd., 828-298-7911 or
    1-800-932-6408)
*Durham 27705 (508 Fulton St., 919-286-0411)
*Fayetteville 28301 (2300 Ramsey St., 910-488-2120)
*Salisbury 28144 (1601 Brenner Ave., 704-638-9000)


***Clinics:***
Charlotte 28262 (Presb. Med. Plaza, 8401 Medical Ctr. Dr., Suite
    350, 704-547-0020)
Durham 27705 (1824 Hill and Dale Rd., 919-383-6107)
Greenville 27858 (800 Moye Blvd., 252-830-2149)
Jacksonville 28540 (1021 Hargett St., 910-219-1339)
Morehead City 28557 (5420 Highway 70, 252-240-2349)
Raleigh 27610 (23 Sunnybrook Rd., Suite 107, 919-212-0129)
Wilmington 28401 (1606 Physicians Dr., Suite 104, 910-362-8811)
Winston-Salem 27103 (190 Kimel Park Dr., 336-768-3296, extension
    1209 or extension 1210)
***Regional Office:***
Winston-Salem 27155 (Federal Bldg., 251 N. Main St., statewide
    1-800-827-1000, nationwide Loan Guaranty Certificate of
    Eligibility Center 1-888-244-6711)
***Vet Centers:***
Charlotte 28202 (223 S. Brevard St., Suite 103, 704-333-6107)
Fayetteville 28311 (4140 Ramsey St., Suite 110, 910-488-6252)
Greensboro 27406 (2009 S. Elm-Eugene St., 336-333-5366)
Greenville 27858 (150 Arlington Blvd., Suite B, 252-355-7920)
Raleigh 27604 (1649 Old Louisburg Rd., 919-856-4616)

**National Cemeteries:**
New Bern NC 28560 (1711 National Ave., 252-637-2912)
Raleigh NC 27610-3335 (501 Rock Quarry Rd., 252-637-2912)
Salisbury NC 28144 (202 Government Rd., 704-636-2661/4621)
Wilmington NC 28403 (2011 Market St., 252-637-2912)

# NORTH DAKOTA
**Medical Center:**
*Fargo 58102 (2101 N. Elm St., 701-232-3241)
**Clinics:**
Bismarck 58503 (Gateway Mall, 2700 State St., Suite 5,
    701-221-9169)
Grafton 58237 (West 6th St., 701-352-4059)
Minot 58705 (10 Missile Ave., 701-727-9800)
**Regional Office:**
Fargo 58102 (2101 Elm St., statewide 1-800-827-1000)
**Vet Centers:**
Bismarck 58501 (1684 Capital Way, 701-224-9751)
Fargo 58103 (3310 Fiechtner Dr., Suite 100, 701-237-0942)
Minot 58701 (2041 3rd St. N.W., 701-852-0177)

# OHIO
**Medical Centers:**
#*Brecksville 44141 (10000 Brecksville Rd., 440-526-3030)
*Chillicothe 45601 (17273 State Route 104, 740-773-1141)
#*Cincinnati 45220 (3200 Vine St., 513-861-3100)
Cleveland 44106, (10701 East Blvd., 216-791-3800)
#*Dayton 45428 (4100 W. 3rd St., 937-268-6511)

**Clinics:**
Akron 44319-1116 (55 W. Waterloo, 330-724-7715)
Ashtabula 44004 (1230 Lake Ave., 440-964-6454)
Athens 45701 (510 W. Union St., 740-593-7314)
Cambridge 43727 (2146 Southgate Pkwy., 740-432-1963)
Canton 44702 (733 Market Ave., S., 330-489-4600)
Cincinnati 45245 (Eastgate Prof. Bldg. 4355 Ferguson Dr., Suite 270,
    513-943-3680)
Cleveland/McCafferty 44113 (4242 Lorain Ave., 216-939-0699)
Columbus 43203 (543 Taylor Ave., 614-257-5200)
East Liverpool 43920 (332 W. 6th St., 330-386-4303)
Georgetown 45121 (4903 State Route 125, 937-378-3413)

Grove City 43123 (1955 Ohio Dr., 614-257-5800)
Hamilton 45011 (1755C S. Erie Hwy., 513-870-9744)
Lancaster 43130 (Colonnade Med. Bldg, 1550 Sheridan Dr.,
    740-653-6145)
Lima 45804 (1303 Bellefontaine Ave., 419-222-5788)
Lorain 44052 (205 W. 20th St., 440-244-3833)
Mansfield 44906 (1456 Park Avenue West, 419-529-4602)
Marietta 45750 (418 Colegate Dr., 740-568-0412)
Marion 43302 (1203 Delaware Ave., 614-257-5920)
Middletown 45042 (675 N. University Blvd., 513-423-8387)
New Philadelphia 44663 (1260 Monroe Ave., 15H, 330-602-5339)
Newark 43055 (1912 Tamarck Rd., 740-788-8329)
Painesville 44077 (7 West Jackson St., 440-357-6740)
Portsmouth 45662 (621 Broadway St., 740-353-3236)
Ravenna 44266 (6751 N. Chestnut St., 330-296-3641)
St. Clairsville 43950 (107 Plaza Dr., Suite 0, 740-695-9321)
Sandusky 44870 (3416 Columbus Ave., 419-625-7350)
Springfield 45505 (512 S. Burnett Rd., 937-328-3385)
Toledo 43614 (3333 Glendale Ave., 419-259-2000)
Warren 44485 (Riverside Sq., 1400 Tod Ave. NW, 330-392-0311)
Youngstown 44505 (2031 Belmont Ave., 330-740-9200)
Zanesville 43701 (840 Bethesda Dr., Bldg., 3-A, 740-453-7725)

**Regional Office:**
Cleveland 44199 (Anthony J. Celebrezze Fed. Bldg., 1240 E. 9th St.,
    1-800-827-1000)

**Benefits Offices:**
Cincinnati 45202 (36 E. Seventh St., Suite 210, 1-800-827-1000)
Columbus 43215 (Federal Bldg., Rm. 309, 200 N. High St.,
    1-800-827-1000)
**Vet Centers:**
Cincinnati 45203 (801-B W. 8th St., 513-763-3500)
Cleveland Heights 44118 (2022 Lee Rd., 216-932-8471)
Columbus 43215 (30 Spruce St., 614-257-5550)
Dayton 45402 (111 W 1st St., Suite 101, 937-461-9150)
Parma 44129 (5700 Pearl Rd., Suite 102, 440-845-5023)
**National Cemeteries:**
Dayton NC 45428-1008 (4100 W. Third St., 937-262-2115)
Ohio Western Reserve NC 44270 (P.O. Box 8, 10175 Rawiga Rd.,
    Rittman, 330-335-3069)

## OKLAHOMA
***Medical Centers:***
Muskogee 74401 (1011 Honor Heights Dr., 918-683-3261)
*Oklahoma City 73104 (921 N.E. 13th St., 405-270-0501)
***Clinics:***
Ardmore 73401 (1015 S. Commerce, 580-223-2266)
Clinton 73601 (1/4 mile south of I-40 on Highway 183)
Lawton/Fort Sill 73503 (Bldg. 4303, 4303 Pittman and Thomas,
    580-353-1131)
McAlester 74501 (903 E. Monroe St., 918-423-2880)
Ponca City 74601 (215 N. 3rd, 580-762-1777)
Seminole Co. 74849 (Konawa, 527 W. Third St., 580-925-3286)
Tulsa 74145 (9322 E. 41st St., 918-764-7243)
***Regional Office:***
Muskogee 74401 (Federal Bldg., 125 S. Main St., 1-800-827-1000)
***Benefits Office:***
Oklahoma City 73102 (Federal Campus, 301 NW 6th St., Suite 113,
    1-800-827-1000)
***Vet Centers:***
Oklahoma City 73105 (3033 N. Walnut, Suite 101W, 405-270-5184)
Tulsa 74112 (1408 S. Harvard, 918-748-5105)
***National Cemeteries:***
Fort Gibson NC 74434 (1423 Cemetery Rd., 918-478-2334)
Fort Sill NC 73538 (2648 Jake Dunn Rd., 580-492-3200)


## OREGON
***Medical Centers:***
#*Portland 97239 (3710 S.W. U.S. Veterans Hospital Rd.,
    503-220-8262)
*Roseburg 97470 (913 N.W. Garden Valley Blvd., 541-440-1000)
***Clinics:***
Bandon 97411 (1010 1st St. S.E., Suite 100, 541-347-4736)
Bend 97701 (2115 Wyatt Court, Suite 201, 1-888-233-8305)
Brookings 97415 (555 5th St., 541-412-1152)
Eugene 97404 (100 River Ave., 541-607-0897)
Klamath Falls 97601 (2819 Dahlia St, 541-273-6206/6129)
Salem 97301 (1660 Oak St., SE, 1-888-233-8305)
Warrenton 97146 (Camp Rilea, 91400 Rilea Neocoxie Rd., Bldg.
    7315, 1-888-233-8305)
***Rehabilitation Center:***
White City 97503 (8495 Crater Lake Hwy., 541-826-2111, ext. 3210

or 3239, 1-800-809-8725)
**Regional Office:**
Portland 97204 (Edith Green/Wendell Wyatt Federal Building, 1220
   S.W. Third Ave., 1-800-827-1000)
**Vet Centers:**
Eugene 97403 (1255 Pearl St., 541-465-6918)
Grants Pass 97526 (211 S.E. 10th St., 541-479-6912)
Portland 97220 (8383 N.E. Sandy Blvd., Suite 110, 503-273-5370)
Salem 97301 (617 Chemeketa St., N.E., 503-362-9911)
**National Cemeteries:**
Eagle Point NC 97524 (2763 Riley Rd., 541-826-2511)
Roseburg NC 97470 (913 Garden Valley Blvd, 541-826-2511)
Willamette NC 97266-6937 (11800 S.E. Mt. Scott Blvd., Portland,
   503-273-5250)


# PENNSYLVANIA
**Medical Centers:**
*Altoona 16602 (2907 Pleasant Valley Blvd., 814-943-8164 or
   877-626-2500)
#*Butler 16001 (325 New Castle Rd., 724-287-4781 or
   1-800-362-8262)
#*Coatesville 19320 (1400 Black Horse Hill Rd., 610-384-7711 or
   1-800-290-6172)
*Erie 16504-1596 (135 E. 38th St., 814-868-8661 or
   1-800-274-8387)
*Lebanon 17042 (1700 S. Lincoln Ave., 717-272-6621, toll free
   1-800-409-8771)
*Philadelphia 19104 (University & Woodland Aves., 215-823-5800
   or 1-800-949-1001)
Pittsburgh Health Care System:
   Pittsburgh 15240 (University Dr., 412-688-6000 or
   1-866-482-7488)
*Wilkes-Barre 18711 (1111 East End Blvd., 570-824-3521 or
   1-877-928-2621)
**Clinics:**
Aliquippa 15001 (2360 Hospital Dr., 724-857-0424)
Allentown 18103 (3100 Hamilton Blvd., 610-776-4304 or
   1-866-249-6472)
Bangor 18013 (701 Slate Belt Blvd., 610-599-0127)
Berwick 18603 (301 West 3rd St., 570-759-0351)
Camp Hill 17011 (25 N. 32nd St., 717-730-9782)

DuBois 15801 (190 West Park Ave., Suite 8, 814-375-6817 or
    1-866-662-0447)
Ellwood City 16117 (Medical Arts Bldg., 304 Evans Dr.,
    724-285-2203)
Foxburg 16049 (855 Route 58, Suite 1, 724-659-5601)
Frackville 17931 (10 East Spruce St., 570-874-4289)
Greensburg 15601 (Hempfield Plaza, Rt. 30, 724-837-5200)
Hermitage 16148 (295 N. Kerrwood Dr., Suite 110, 724-346-1569)
Johnstown 15904 (University Park Plaza, 1425 Scalp Ave., Suite 29,
    814-266-8696)
Kittanning 16201 (ACMH, 1 Nolte Dr., 724-543-8711)
Lancaster 17601 (Greenfield Corporate Center, 1861 Charter Lane,
    Suite 118, 717-290-6900)
Meadville 16335 (18955 Park Avenue Plaza, 814-337-0170)
New Castle 16101 (Jameson South Campus, 1000 S. Mercer St.,
    724-285-2203)
Oil City 16301 (174 Bissell Ave., 814-678-2631)
Pottsville 17901 (700 Schuylkill Manor Rd., 570-621-4115)
Reading 19601 (145 N. Sixth St., 3rd Fl., St. Jos. Med. Comm.
    Camp., 610-208-4717)
Sayre 18840 (1537 Elmira St., 570-888-6803 or 1-877-470-0920)
Shippenville 16254 (Marianne Family Practice, 21159 Paint Blvd.,
    Suite 2, 814-226-6770)
State College 16801-2755 (3048 Enterprise Dr., Ferguson Sq.
    Bldg., 1, 814-867-5415)
Smethport 16749 (406 Franklin St, 814-887-5655)
Spring City 19475 (11 Independence Dr., 610-948-1082)
Springfield 19064 (194 W. Sproul Rd., Suite 105, Crozier Keystone
Healthplex, 610-543-3246)
Tobyhanna 18466 (Bldg. 220, Tobyhanna Army Depot,
    570-895-8341)
Uniontown 15401 (404 W. Main St., 724-439-4990)
Warren 16365 (3 Farm Colony Dr., 814-723-9763)
Washington 15301 (100 Ridge Ave., 724-250-7790)
Williamsport 17701 (Divine Providence, Suite 304, 1705 Warren
    Ave., 570-322-4791)
Willow Grove/Horsham 19044 (433 Caredean, 215-823-6050)
York 17403 (1796 3rd Ave., 717-854-2481)

***Regional Offices:***
Philadelphia 19101 (Regional Office and Insurance Center,
    P.O. Box 8079, 5000 Wissahickon Ave., 1-800-827-1000;
Serves counties of Adams, Berks, Bradford, Bucks, Cameron,

Carbon, Centre, Chester, Clinton, Columbia, Dauphin, Dela
ware, Franklin, Juniata, Lackawanna, Lancaster, Leba-
non, Lehigh, Luzerne, Lycoming, Mifflin, Monroe, Montgom-
ery, Montour, Northampton, Northumberland, Perry, Philadelphia,
Pike, Potter, Schuylkill, Snyder, Sullivan, Susquehanna,
Tioga, Union, Wayne, Wyoming, York.)
Pittsburgh 15222 (1000 Liberty Ave., statewide 1-800-827-1000.
Serves remaining counties of Pennsylvania.)

**Benefits Office:**
Wilkes-Barre 18702 (1123 East End Blvd., Bldg. 35, Suite 11,
1-800-827-1000)


**Vet Centers:**
Erie 16501 (1000 State St., Suite 1&2, 814-453-7955)
Harrisburg 17102 (1500 N. 2nd St., Suite 2, 717-782-3954)
McKeesport 15131 (2001 Lincoln Way., 412-678-7704)
Philadelphia 19107 (801 Arch St., Suite 102, 215-627-0238)
Philadelphia 19120 (101 E. Olney Ave., 215-924-4670)
Pittsburgh 15205 (2500 Baldwick Rd., Suite 15, 412-920-1765)
Scranton 18505 (1002 Pittston Ave., 570-344-2676)
Williamsport 17701 (805 Penn St., 570-327-5281)

**National Cemeteries:**
Indiantown Gap NC 17003-9618 (R.R. 2, P.O. Box 484, Annville,
717-865-5254)
NC of the Alleghenies 15017 (1158 Morgan Rd., Bridgeville,
724-746-4363)
Philadelphia NC 19138 (Haines St. & Limekiln Pike, 609-877-5460)


# PHILIPPINES
**Regional Office:**
Manila 0930 (1131 Roxas Blvd., 011-632-528-6300, International
Mailing Address: PSC 501, FPO AP 96515-1100)

**Clinic:**
Manila (2201 Roxas Blvd., Pasay City, 1300 Philippines,
011-632-833-4566, International Mailing Address PSC 501, FPO
AP 96515-1100)


# PUERTO RICO
**Medical Center:**
*San Juan 00921-3201 (10 Casia St., 787-641-7582 or
1-800-449-8729)

## Clinics:

Arecibo 00612 (Victor Rojas 2, Zona Industrial Carr 9, 787-816-1818 or 1-866-874-6569)

Guayama 00784 (FISA Building-First Floor, Paseo del Pueblo, Km. 0.3, Lote No. 6, 787-866-8766)

Mayaguez 00680-1507 (Avenida Hostos #345, 787-834-6900)

Ponce 00716-2001 (Paseo del Veterano #1010, 787-812-3163 or 1-800-563-5086)

## Regional Office:

San Juan 00918-1703 (150 Carlos Chardon Ave., Suite 300. Send mail to Suite 232. Serving all Puerto Rico and the Virgin Islands, 1-800-827-1000)

## Benefits Offices:

Mayaguez 00680-1507 (Ave. Hostos 345, Carretera 2, Frente al Centro Medico, 1-800-827-1000)

Ponce 00731 (10 Paseo del Veterano, 1-800-827-1000)

Arecibo 00612 (Gonzalo Marin 50, 1-800-827-1000)

## Vet Centers:

Arecibo 00612-4702 (52 Gonzalo Marin St., 787-879-4510/4581)

Ponce 00731 (35 Mayo St., 787-841-3260)

San Juan 00921 (Condominio Med. Ctr. Plaza, Suite LC8A11, La Riviera, 787-749-4409)

## National Cemetery:

Puerto Rico NC 00960 (Ave. Cementerio Nacional 50, Barrio Hato Tejas, Bayamon, 787-798-8400)

# RHODE ISLAND

## Medical Center:

Providence 02908 (830 Chalkstone Ave., 401-273-7100)

## Clinic:

Middletown 02842 (One Corporate Pl., West Main Rd., 401-847-6239)

## Regional Office:

Providence 02903 (380 Westminster St.; statewide, 1-800-827-1000)

## Vet Center:

Warwick 02889 (2038 Warwick Ave., 401-739-0167)

# SOUTH CAROLINA

## Medical Centers:

*Charleston 29401 (109 Bee St., 843-577-5011)

*Columbia 29209-1639 (6439 Garners Ferry Rd., 803-776-4000)

*Clinics:*
Anderson 29621 (1702 East Greenville St., 864-224-5450)
Beaufort 29902 (1 Pinckney Blvd., 843-770-0444)
Florence 29501 (805 Pamplico Highway, Suite 220A, 843-292-8383)
Goose Creek 29406 (9237 University Blvd. North, 843-789-6400)
Greenville 29605 (3510 Augusta Rd., 864-299-1600)
Myrtle Beach 29577 (3381 Phillis Blvd., 843-477-0177)
Orangeburg 29118 (1767 Village Park Dr., 803-533-1335)
Rock Hill 29732 (205 Piedmont Blvd., 803-366-4848)
Sumter 29150 (407 N. Salem St., 803-938-9901)
*Nursing Home:*
Walterboro 29488 (2461 Sidneys Road, Veterans Victory House,
    843-538-3000)
*Regional Office:*
Columbia 29201 (1801 Assembly St., statewide 1-800-827-1000)
*Vet Centers:*
Columbia 29201 (1513 Pickens St., 803-765-9944)
Greenville 29601 (14 Lavinia Ave., 864-271-2711)
North Charleston 29406 (5603-A Rivers Ave., 843-747-8387)
*National Cemeteries:*
Beaufort NC  29902-3947 (1601 Boundary St., 843-524-3925)
Florence NC 29501 (803 E. National Cemetery Rd., 843-669-8783)

## SOUTH DAKOTA
*Medical Centers:*
Black Hills Health Care System:
    *Fort Meade 57741 (113 Comanche Rd., 605-347-2511 or
    1-800-743-1070)
    #Hot Springs 57747 (500 N. 5th St., 605-745-2000 or
    1-800-764-5370)
*Sioux Falls 57105 (2501 W. 22nd St., 605-336-3230)
*Clinics:*
Aberdeen 57401 (1440 15th Ave NW, 605-622-2640)
Eagle Butte 57625 (315 Main St., 605-964-8000)
Isabel 57633 (118 N. Main St., 605-466-2120)
Faith 57626 (112 N. 2nd Ave., 605-967-2644)
Mission/Rosebud 57570 (153 S. Main St., 605-856-2295 or
    1-800-764-5370)
Pierre 57501 (1601 N. Harrison, Suite 6, 605-945-1710)
Rapid City 57701 (3625 5th St., 605-718-1095 or 1-800-743-1070)
Winner 57580 (915 E. 8th St., 605-745-2000, ext. 2474)

McLauglin TWS 57642 (302 Sale Barn Rd., 605-823-4574 or
    1-800-743-1070)
**Regional Office:**
Sioux Falls 57117 (P.O. Box 5046, 2501 W. 22nd St., statewide
    1-800-827-1000)
**Vet Centers:**
Martin 57551 (East Hwy 18, 605-685-1300)
Rapid City 57701 (621 6th St., Suite 101 Kansas City St.,
    605-348-0077)
Sioux Falls 57104 (601 S. Cliff Ave., Suite C, 605-330-4552)
**National Cemeteries:**
Black Hills NC 57785 (20901 Pleasant Valley Dr., Sturgis,
    605-347-3830)
Fort Meade NC 57785 (P.O. Box 640, Old Stone Rd., Sturgis,
    605-347-3830)
Hot Springs NC 57747 (500 N 5th St., 605-347-3830)


## TENNESSEE
**Medical Centers:**
*Memphis 38104 (1030 Jefferson Ave., 901-523-8990)
#*Mountain Home 37684 (P.O. Box 4000, 423-926-1171)
VA Tennessee Valley Healthcare System:
    Nashville Campus 37212 (1310 24th Ave., South, 615-327-4751)
    Alvin C. York Campus, Murfreesboro 37129 (3400 Lebanon Pike,
    615-867-6000)
**Clinics:**
Chattanooga 37411 (150 Debra Rd., Suite 5200, Bldg 6200,
    423-893-6500)
Clarksville 37043 (Gateway Med. Ctr., Suite 110, 1731 Memorial St.,
    931-221-2171)
Cookeville 38501 (Primary Care, 1101 Neal St., 931-525-1652)
Covington 38128 (3461 Austin Peay Hwy., 901-261-4500)
Dover 37058-0497 (1021 Spring St., PO Box 497, 931-232-5329)
Knoxville 37923 (9031 Cross Park Dr., 865-545-4592)
Memphis South 38116 (1056 East Raines Rd., 901-271-4900)
Mountain City 37683 (PO Box 738, 423-727-1103)
Nashville/Vine Hill Clinic 37204 (601 Benton Ave., 615-292-9770)
Rogersville 37857 (PO Box 850, 423-272-5600)
Savannah 38372 (765-A Florence Rd., 731-925-2300)
Smithville 38870 (63420 Highway 25 N., 901-523-8990)
Tullahoma 37389 (Arnold AFB, 225 First St., 931-454-6134)

**Regional Office:**
Nashville 37203 (110 9th Ave., South, statewide 1-800-827-1000)
**Vet Centers:**
Chattanooga 37411 (951 Eastgate Loop Rd., Bldg. 5700, Suite 300,
    423-855-6570)
Johnson City 37604 (1615A W. Market St., 423-928-8387)
Knoxville 37914 (2817 E. Magnolia Ave., 865-545-4680)
Memphis 38104 (1835 Union, Suite 100, 901-544-0173)
Nashville 37217 (Airpark Bus. Cen. 1, Suite A-5, 1420 Donelson
    Pike, 615-366-1220)
**National Cemeteries:**
Chattanooga NC 37404 (1200 Bailey Ave., 423-855-6590)
Knoxville NC 37917 (939 Tyson St., N.W., 423-855-6590)
Memphis NC 38122 (3568 Townes Ave., 901-386-8311)
Mountain Home NC 37684 (P.O. Box 8, VAMC, Bldg. 117,
    423-979-3535)
Nashville NC 37115-4619 (1420 Gallatin Rd. So., Madison,
    615-860-0086)


# TEXAS
**Medical Centers:**
*Amarillo 79106 (6010 Amarillo Blvd., West, 806-355-9703 or
    1-800-687-8262)
El Paso Hlth. Care Sys. 79930 (5001 N. Piedras St., 915-564-6100,
    1-800-672-3782)
*Houston 77030 (2002 Holcombe Blvd., 713-791-1414)
West Texas Health Care System
    *Big Spring 79720 (300 Veterans Blvd., 432-263-7361 or
    1-800-472-1365)
Central Texas Health Care System:
    #*Temple 76504 (1901 Veterans Memorial Dr., 800-423-2111
    or 254-778-4811)
    Waco 76711 (4800 Memorial Dr., 254-752-6581 or
    1-800-423-2111)
North Texas Health Care System:
    #*Bonham 75418 (1201 East Ninth St., 800-924-8387)
    #*Dallas 75216 (4500 S. Lancaster Rd., 800-849-3597)
South Texas Health Care System:
    *San Antonio 78229-4404 (7400 Merton Minter Blvd.,
    210-617-5300)
    *Kerrville 78028 (3600 Memorial Blvd., 830-896-2020)

## Clinics:

Abilene 78606 (4225 Woods Place, 325-695-3252)
Aledo 76008 (317 FM 1187 North, 1-800-924-8387)
Alice/Christus Spohn San Diego 78384 (215 Dr. E.E. Dunlap St.,
    361-279-3378)
Austin 78741 (2901 Montopolis Dr., 512-389-1010)
Beaumont 77707 (3420 Veteran Circle, 409-981-8550)
Beeville 78102 (Family Practice, 302 South Hillside Dr.,
    361-358-9912)
Bonham/Red River (Grayson, Delta, and Lamar Counties, 800-924-
8387, ext. 36676 or 903-583-6676)
Bridgeport 76426 (808 Woodrow Wilson Ray Cir., 940-683-2538)
Brownwood 76801 (2600 Memorial Park Dr., 325-641-0568)
Cedar Park 78613 (701 E. Whitestone Blvd., 512-260-1368)
Childress 79201 (Highway 83 North, 940-937-3636)
Cleburne (Johnson and Ellis Counties, 800-924-8387 ext. 36674
    or 903-583-6674)
College Station/Bryan 77845 (1605 Rock Prairie Rd., Suite 212,
    979-680-0361)
Corpus Christi 78405 (5283 Old Brownsville Rd., 361-806-5600)
Decatur 76426 (Wise, Jack, Clay, Archer, Baylor, Young, Throckmor-
ton and Montague Counties, 800-924-8387 ext. 6674 or 903-583-
6674)
Denton 76201 (3537 Interstate 35E, 1-800-924-8387, x36676 or
    903-583-6676)
Eastland (Eastland, Parker, Palo Pinto, Hood, Callahan and Ste-
phens Counties, 1-800-924-8387 ext. 36674 or 903-583-6674)
Fort Stockton 79735 (501 N. Main St., 432-336-0700)
Fort Worth 76104 (300 W. Rosedale St., 1-800-443-9672)
Galveston 77551 (1101 61st St., 1-800-310-5001)
Granbury 76049 (2006 Fall Creek Hwy., 817-326-3440)
Greenville (4311 Wesley St., 903-583-6674)
Harlingen 78550 (1629 Treasure Hills Blvd., Suite 5-B,
    956-366-4500)
Kingsville/Christus Spohn Bishop 78343 (301 West Main,
    361-584-2563)
Laredo 78041 (6551 Star Ct., 956-523-7850)
Longview 75601 (1205 E. Marshall Ave., 903-247-8262)
Lubbock 79412 (6104 Avenue Q South Dr., 806-472-3400)
Lufkin 75904 (1301 W. Frank Ave., 936-637-1342)
Marlin 76661 (1016 Ward St., 1-800-423-2111)
McAllen 78503 (2101 S. Colonel Rowe Blvd., 956-618-7100)

New Braunfels 78130 (Rural Clinic, 189 E. Austin St., Suite 106,
    830-629-3614)
Odessa 79761 (4241 N. Tanglewood Ln., 432-550-0152)
Palestine 75801 (2000 S. Loop 256, Suite 200, 903-723-9006)
Paris 75462 (635 Stone Ave., 903-583-2111)
Red River Co. 75462 (800-924-8387 ext. 36342 or 903-583-6342)
San Angelo 76905 (2018 Pulliam, 325-658-6138)
San Antonio 78240 (Frank M. Tejeda Clinic, 5788 Eckert Rd.,
    210-699-2100)
San Antonio/General McMullen 78226 (1831 General McMullen,
    210-434-1400)
San Antonio/Greenway 78217 (2455 NE Loop 410, Suite 100,
    210-599-6000)
San Antonio/Northern Hills 78217 (13909 Nacogdoches, Suite 124,
    210-653-8989)
San Antonio/Pecan Valley 78222 (4243 E. Southcross, Suite 205,
    210-304-3500)
Seguin 78130 (510 E. Court St., 830-629-3614)
Sherman 75090 (2612 N. Loy Lake, Suite 300, 903-891-8317)
South Bexar Co. 78223 (1055 Ada, San Antonio, 210-358-5701)
Stamford 79553 (1303 Mabee Dr., 325-773-5733)
Stratford 79084 (1220 Purnell St., 806-396-5583)
Tarrant Co. 76107 (call 1-800-924-8387 ext. 36676 or 903-583-6676)
Texas City 77591 (9300 Emmett F. Lowry Expressway, Suite 206,
    409-986-1129 or 1-800-310-5001)
Tyler 75701 (3414 Golden Rd., call 1-800-924-8387 ext. 36674 or
    903-583-6674)
Uvalde 78801 (137 W. Nopal, 830-279-0535)
Victoria 77901 (1502 E. Airline, Suite 40, 361-582-7700)
Waxahachie 75165 (201 Ferris Ave., 972-937-1613)
Wichita Falls 76301 (1800 7th St., 940-723-2373)
### *Regional Offices:*
Houston 77030 (6900 Almeda Rd., statewide, 1-800-827-1000.
    Serves counties of Angelina, Aransas, Atacosa, Austin, Bandera,
    Bee, Bexar, Blanco, Brazoria, Brewster, Brooks, Caldwell,
    Calhoun, Cameron, Chambers, Colorado, Comal, Crockett,
    DeWitt, Dimitt, Duval, Edwards, Fort Bend, Frio, Galveston,
    Gillespie, Goliad, Gonzales, Grimes, Guadeloupe, Hardin,
    Harris, Hays, Hidalgo, Houston, Jackson, Jasper, Jefferson,
    Jim Hogg, Jim Wells, Karnes, Kendall, Kennedy, Kerr,
    Kimble, Kinney, Kleberg, LaSalle, Lavaca, Liberty, Live
    Oak, McCulloch, McMullen, Mason, Matagorda, Maverlck,

Medina, Menard, Montgomery, Nacogdoches, Newton, Nueces, Orange, Pecos, Polk, Real, Refugio, Sabine, San Augustine, San Jacinto, San Patricio, Schleicher, Shelby, Starr, Sutton, Terrell, Trinity, Tyler, Uvalde, Val Verde, Victoria, Walker, Waller, Washington, Webb, Wharton, Willacy, Wilson, Zapata, Zavala)
Waco 76799 (One Veterans Plaza, 701 Clay; statewide, 1-800-827-1000; serves the rest of the state.  In Bowie County, the City of Texarkana is served by Little Rock, AR, VA Regional Office, 1-800-827-1000.)

## Benefits Offices:
Abilene 79602 (Taylor County Plaza Bldg., Suite 103, 400 Oak St., 1-800-827-1000)
Amarillo 79106 (6010 Amarillo Blvd. W., 1-800-827-1000)
Austin 78741 (2901 Montopolis Dr., Room 108, 1-800-827-1000)
Corpus Christi 78405 (4646 Corona Dr., Suite 150, 1-800-827-1000)
Dallas 75216 (4500 S. Lancaster Rd., 1-800-827-1000)
El Paso 79930 (5001 Piedras Dr., 1-800-827-1000)
Ft. Worth 76104-4856 (300 W. Rosedale St., 1-800-827-1000)
Lubbock 79410 (4902 34th St., Suite 10, Rm. 134, 1-800-827-1000)
McAllen 78503 (1901 South 1st St., Suite 400, 1-800-827-1000)
San Antonio 78240 (5788 Eckert Rd., 1-800-827-1000)
Temple 76504 (1901 Veterans Memorial Dr., Room 5G38 [BRB], 1-800-827-1000)
Tyler 75701 (1700 SSE Loop 323, Suite 310, 1-800-827-1000)

## Vet Centers:
Amarillo 79109 (3414 Olsen Blvd., Suite E., 806-354-9779)
Austin 78745 (1110 W. Will Cannon Dr., Suite 301, 512-416-1314)
Corpus Christi 78411 (4646 Corona, Suite 250, 361-854-9961)
Dallas 75231 (10501 N. Central Expressway, Suite 213, 214-361-5896)
El Paso 79925 (1155 Westmoreland, Suite 121, 915-772-0013)
Fort Worth 76104 (1305 W. Magnolia, Suite B, 817-921-9095)
Houston 77006 (503 Westheimer, 713-523-0884)
Houston 77024 (701 N. Post Oak Rd., Suite 102, 713-682-2288)
Laredo 78041 (6020 McPherson Rd., 1A, 956-723-4680)
Lubbock 79410 (3208 34th St., 806-792-9782)
McAllen 78504 (801 Nolana, Suite 140, 956-631-2147)
Midland 79703 (3404 W. Illinois, Suite 1, 915-697-8222)
San Antonio 78212 (231 W. Cypress St., Suite 100, 210-472-4025)

***National Cemeteries:***
Dallas-Fort Worth NC 75211 (2000 Mountain Creek Parkway,
    214-467-3374)
Fort Bliss NC 79906 (Box 6342, 5200 Fred Wilson Rd.,
    915-564-0201)
Fort Sam Houston NC 78209 (1520 Harry Wurzbach Rd., San
    Antonio, 210-820-3891/3894)
Houston NC 77038 (10410 Veterans Memorial Dr., 281-447-8686)
Kerrville NC 78028 (VAMC, 3600 Memorial Blvd.,
    210-820-3891/3894)
San Antonio NC 78202 (517 Paso Hondo St., 210-820-3891/3894)

# UTAH
***Medical Center:***
VA Salt Lake City Health System
    Salt Lake City 84148 (500 Foothill Dr., 801-582-1565 or 1-800-
    613-4012)

***Clinics:***
Fountain Green 84632 (300 W. 300 S., 435-623-3129 ext. 2975)
Nephi 84648 (48 W. 1500 N., 435-623-3129 ext. 2975)
Ogden 84403 (982 Chambers St., 801-479-4105)
Orem 84057 (Timpanogos Regional Hospital, 740 W. 800 North,
    Suite 440, 4th Fl., 801-235-0953 ext. 6250)
Roosevelt 84066 (210 West 300 North (75-3), 435-725-2082)
St. George 84770 (1067 E. Tabernacle, 435-634-7608 ext. 6000)
Regional Office:
Salt Lake City 84158 (P.O. Box 581900, 550 Foothill Dr., statewide
    1-800-827-1000)
***Vet Centers:***
Provo 84601 (750 North 200 West, Suite 105, 801-377-1117)
Salt Lake City 84106 (1354 East 3300 South, 801-584-1294)

# VERMONT
***Medical Center:***
White River Junction 05009 (215 N. Main St., 802-295-9363)
***Clinics:***
Bennington 05201 (Vermont Veterans Home, 325 North St.,
    802-447-6913)
Colchester 05446 (162 Hegeman Ave., Unit 100, 802-655-1356)
Rutland 05702 (215 Stratton Rd., 802-773-3386)

### Regional Office:
White River Junction 05009 (215 N. Main St., 802-296-5177 or
    1-800-827-1000 from within Vermont)
### Vet Centers:
South Burlington 05403 (359 Dorset St., 802-862-1806)
White River Junction 05001 (Gilman Office Complex 2,
    802-295-2908 or 1-800-649-6603)


## VIRGINIA
### Medical Centers:
#*Hampton 23667 (100 Emancipation Dr., 757-722-9961)
*Richmond 23249 (1201 Broad Rock Blvd., 804-675-5000)
*Salem 24153 (1970 Roanoke Blvd., 540-982-2463)
### Clinics:
Alexandria 22309 (8796 D Sacramento Dr., 703-360-1442)
Danville 24541 (Southside Family Medical Center, 100 Vicar Pl.,
    434-836-2100)
Fredericksburg 22401 (1965 Jeff. Davis Hwy., 540-370-4468)
Harrisonburg 22802 (101 North Main St., Suite 220 Harrison Plaza,
    540-442-1773)
Norton 24273 (340 Anderson Hollow Rd., 276-679-5880)
Saltville 24370 (308 W. Main St., 276-496-4433)
St. Charles 24282 (PO Drawer S, 276-383-4487)
Stephens City 22655 (106 Hyde Court, 540-869-0600)
Tazewell 24651 (Tazewell Family Physicians, PO Box 645,
    276-988-2526)
### Regional Office:
Roanoke 24011 (210 Franklin Rd., S.W., statewide 1-800-827-1000)
### Vet Centers:
Alexandria 22309 (8796 Sacramento Dr., Suite D&E, 703-360-8633)
Norfolk 23517 (2200 Colonial Ave., Suite 3, 757-623-7584)
Richmond 23230 (4902 Fitzhugh Ave., 804-353-8958)
Roanoke 24016 (350 Albemarle Ave., SW, 540-342-9726)
### National Cemeteries:
Alexandria NC 22314 (1450 Wilkes St., 703-221-2183/2184)
Balls Bluff NC 22075 (Rte. 7, Leesburg, 540-825-0027)
City Point NC 23860 (10th Ave. & Davis St., Hopewell,
    804-795-2031)
Cold Harbor NC 23111 (Rt. 156 North, Mechanicsville,
    804-795-2031)
Culpeper NC 22701 (305 U.S. Ave., 540-825-0027)

Danville NC 24541 (721 Lee St., 704-636-2661)
Fort Harrison NC 23231 (8620 Varina Rd., Richmond, 804-795-2031)
Glendale NC 23231 (8301 Willis Church Rd., Richmond,
    804-795-2031)
Hampton NC 23667 (Cemetery Rd. at Marshall Ave., 757-723-7104)
Hampton NC 23667 (VAMC, Emancipation Dr., 757-723-7104)
Quantico NC 22172 (P.O. Box 10, 18424 Joplin Rd. (Rte. 619),
    703-221-2183/2184)
Richmond NC 23231 (1701 Williamsburg Rd., 804-795-2031)
Seven Pines NC 23150 (400 E. Williamsburg Rd., Sandston,
    804-795-2031)
Staunton NC, 24401 (901 Richmond Ave., 540-825-0027)
Winchester NC 22601 (401 National Ave., 540-825-0027)

## VIRGIN ISLANDS
### *Clinics:*
St. Croix 00850-4701 (Village Mall #113, RR-02, Kingshill,
    340-778-5553)
St. Thomas 00802 (Buchaneer Mall 8, 340-774-6674)
### *Benefits:*
Served by San Juan, Puerto Rico, VA Regional Office,
    1-800-827-1000
### *Vet Centers:*
St. Croix 00850 (Box 12, R.R. 02, Village Mall, 113, RR2 Box 10556,
    Kingshill, 340-778-5553)
St. Thomas 00802 (9800 Buchaneer Mall, Suite 8, 340-774-6674)

## WASHINGTON
### *Medical Centers:*
Puget Sound Health Care System:
    *Seattle 98108 (1660 S. Columbian Way, 206-762-1010)
    #*Tacoma 98493 (9600 Veterans Dr., S.W., American Lake,
    253-582-8440)
*Spokane 99205 (4815 N. Assembly St., 509-434-7000)
*Walla Walla 99362 (77 Wainwright Dr., 509-525-5200)
### *Clinics:*
Bremerton 98310 (925 Adele Ave., 360-782-0129)
Factoria 98006 (13231 SE 36th St., Suite 110, 425-957-9000)
Kent 98032 (23213 Pacific Hwy. South, 206-870-8880)
Tri-Cities 99352 (Richland, 948 Stevens Dr., Suite C, 509-946-1020)
Yakima 98902 (717 Fruitvale Blvd., 509-966-0199)

**Regional Office:**
Seattle 98174 (Fed. Bldg., 915 2nd Ave., statewide 1-800-827-1000)
**Benefits Offices:**
Fort Lewis 98433 (Waller Hall Rm. 700, P.O. Box 331153,
    253-967-7106)
Bremerton 98337 (W. Sound Pre-Separation Center, 262 Burwell St.,
    360-782-9900)
**Vet Centers:**
Bellingham 98226 (3800 Byron Ave., Suite 124, 360-733-9226)
Seattle 98121 (2030 9th Ave., Suite 210, 206-553-2706)
Spokane 99206 (100 N. Mullan Rd., Suite 102, 509-444-8387)
Tacoma 98409 (4916 Center St., Suite E, 253-565-7038)
Yakima 98902 (1111 N. First St., 509-457-2736)
**National Cemetery:**
Tahoma NC 98042-4868 (18600 S.E. 240th St., Kent, 425-413-9614)

## WEST VIRGINIA
**Medical Centers:**
*Beckley 25801 (200 Veterans Ave., 304-255-2121)
Clarksburg 26301 (1 Medical Center Dr., 304-623-3461 or
    1-800-733-0512)
Huntington 25704 (1540 Spring Valley Dr., 304-429-6741)
#*Martinsburg 25401 (510 Butler Ave., 304-263-0811 or
    1-800-817-3807)
**Clinics:**
Charleston 25304 (104 Alex Lane, 304-926-6001)
Franklin 26807 (Pendleton Comm. Care, 314 Pine St.,
    304-358-2355)
Gassaway 26624 (617 River St., 304-364-5654)
Logan 25601 (513 Dingess St., 304-752-8355)
Parkersburg 26101 (912 Market St., 304-422-5114)
Parsons 26287 (206 Spruce St., 304-478-2219)
Petersburg 26847 (c/o Grant Memorial Hospital, Route 55 W.,
    304-257-1026, ext. 120)
Williamson 25661 (75 W. 4th Ave., 304-235-2187)
**Regional Office:**
Huntington 25701 (640 Fourth Ave., statewide 1-800-827-1000;
    counties of Brooke, Hancock, Marshall, Ohio, served by
    Pittsburgh, Pa., VA Regional Office)
**Vet Centers:**
Beckley 25801 (101 Ellison Ave., 304-252-8220)

Charleston 25302 (521 Central Ave., 304-343-3825)
Huntington 25701 (3135 16th St. Rd., Suite 11, 304-523-8387)
#Martinsburg 25401 (900 Winchester Ave., 304-263-6776)
Morgantown 26508 (1083 Greenbag Rd., 304-291-4303)
Princeton 24740 (905 Mercer St., 304-425-5653)
Wheeling 26003 (1206 Chapline St., 304-232-0587)
**National Cemeteries:**
Grafton NC 26354 (431 Walnut St., 304-265-2044)
West Virginia NC 26354 (Rt. 2, Box 127, Grafton, 304-265-2044)


# WISCONSIN
**Medical Centers:**
Madison 53705 (2500 Overlook Terrace, 608-256-1901)
#*Milwaukee 53295 (5000 W. National Ave., 414-384-2000)
*Tomah 54660 (500 E. Veterans St., 608-372-3971)
**Clinics:**
Appleton 54914 (10 Tri-Park Way, 920-831-0070)
Baraboo 53913 (626 14th St., 608-356-9318)
Beaver Dam 53916 (208 LaCrosse St., 920-356-9415)
Chippewa Falls 54729 (2503 County Hwy. I, 715-720-3780)
Cleveland 53015 (1205 North Ave., 920-693-3750)
Green Bay 54303 (141 Siegler St., 920-497-3126)
Janesville 53545 (111 N. Main St. 608-758-9300)
Kenosha 53140 (800 55th St., 262-653-9286)
LaCrosse 54601-3200 (2600 State Rd., 608-784-3886)
Loyal 54446 (PO Box 26, 141 North Main St., 715-255-9799)
Rhinelander 54501 (3716 Country Dr., 6, 715-362-4080)
Superior 54880 (3520 Tower Ave., 715-392-9711)
Union Grove 53182 (21425 Spring St., 262-878-7000)
Wausau 54401 (515 S. 32nd Ave., 715-842-2834)
Wisconsin Rapids 54494 (710 E. Grand Ave., 715-424-3844)
**Regional Office:**
Milwaukee 53214 (5400 W. National Ave., statewide
    1-800-827-1000)
**Vet Centers:**
Madison 53703 (147 S. Butler St., 608-264-5342)
Milwaukee 53218 (5401 N. 76th St., 414-536-1301)
**National Cemetery:**
Wood NC 53295-4000 (5000 W. National Ave., Bldg. 1301,
    Milwaukee, 414-382-5300)

## WYOMING
### Medical Centers
*Cheyenne 82001 (2360 E. Pershing Blvd., 307-778-7550 or
    1-888-483-9127)
*Sheridan 82801 (1898 Fort Rd., 307-672-3473)
### Clinics:
Casper 82601 (4140 S. Poplar St., 307-235-4143)
Gillette 82718 (1701 Phillips Circle, Suite A, 307-685-0676)
Green River 82935 (1400 Uinta Dr., 307-872-4508 ext. 4997)
Newcastle 82701 (1124 Washington Blvd., 307-746-9533 or
    1-800-764-5370)
Powell 82435 (777 Ave. H, 307-754-7257)
Riverton 82501 (2300 Rose Lane, 307-857-1211)
Rock Springs 82901 (3000 College Dr., Suite C, 307-362-6641)
Benefits Office:
Cheyenne 82001 (2360 E. Pershing Blvd., statewide
    1-800-827-1000)
### Vet Centers:
Casper 82601 (111 S. Jefferson, Suite 100, 307-261-5355)
Cheyenne 82001 (2424 Pioneer Ave., Suite 103, 307-778-7370)

# Index

# Federal Benefits for Veterans and Dependents 2007

## Publication ORDER FORM

**Order Processing Code**
**3490**
**Easy Secure Internet:**
**bookstore.gpo.gov**

**Toll Free:** 866 512–1800
**Phone:** 202 512–1800
**Fax:** 202 512–2250

**Mail:**
Superintendent of Documents
PO Box 371954
Pittsburgh, PA 15250–7954

❑ YES! please send me________copies of *Federal Benefits for Veterans and Dependents 2007*. S/N 051–000–00231–8, ISBN: 978–0–16–078005–9, single copies $5.00; $67.00/pack of 25.

❑ YES! please send me________*Beneficios Federales para los Veteranos y sus Dependientes, Edicion 2007*. S/N 051–000–00232–6, ISBN: 978–0–16–078006–6, single copies $5.00; $67.00/pack of 25.

The total cost of my order is $__________. Price includes regular postage and handling and price is subject to change. International customer please add 40%. Price subject to change without notice.

Personal name                                                                 (Please type or print)

Company name

Street address

City, State, Zip code

Daytime phone including area code

*Charge your order, It's easy!*   VISA   MasterCard   DISCOVER/NOVUS   AMERICAN EXPRESS

❑ Check payable to *Superintendent of Documents*

❑ SOD Deposit Account  ⬚⬚⬚⬚⬚⬚⬚ – ⬚

❑ VISA  ❑ MasterCard  ❑ Discover/NOVUS  ❑ American Express

**GPO**
U.S. GOVERNMENT
PRINTING OFFICE
KEEPING AMERICA INFORMED

(expiration date)                                        *Thank you for your order!*

Authorizing signature                                                                 02/07